Foundation of the Fire:

By

Ricky LaVaughn

Using fire as a metaphor in building a relationship with God

LaVauri Publishing House

Foundation of the Fire
Using fire as a metaphor in building a relationship with God
https://www.lavauri.com/foundation.html

Published by LaVauri Publishing House
Printed in the United States of America

Cover Designed by John T. Jones

Other inspirational books by Ricky LaVaughn

In The Beginning: Bible Study on the book of Genesis
The Golden Image

Acknowledgments

First, I have to thank God for the inspiration and gift to write. It was tough writing a non-fictional book, but God has allowed me to get past that and be able to put these ideas into written words.

I would like to thank my editors, Jennifer Talbert and Amanda Post. They helped take this book to a higher standard so all people can have an understanding in building a relationship with Jesus Christ.

In addition, to include my family who have constantly been supportive and helped mold me to become the person I am today.

To all people who said I could do it, thank you so much for your constant prayers and uplifting spirit.

This book is to help you build a personal foundation in God. There are sections to each chapter designed to help you build a strong relationship with Him. Feel free to use all of these resources and more to help you gain a deeper understanding of Jesus Christ.

This is the revised and improved version of Foundation of the Fire. This book is combined with the Workbook and is designed to give you the space and opportunity to take notes while you build a personal relationship with God. This is the new and improved version that includes the book, "Foundation of the Fire." With this version, you are now able to have the book the Workbook follows all in one guide.

There are certain areas in this book that will help you with your study.

1.) ***Chapter from Foundation of the Fire:*** Here is the part of the chapter from "Foundation of the Fire." It is a part of your base as well as The Holy Bible. Read this section to help answer the questions in the Study Guide and build a closer relationship with God. Each chapter contains; the suggested scripture, a quote from the Bible, the chapter itself, a list of quoted scriptures, and a list of scriptures for future study.

2.) ***Study Guide:*** The first part are questions that go along with the chapter. Sometimes you will see a direct Biblical scripture to help you find the answer or a page number that corresponds to "Foundation of the Fire (FOTF)." Not all questions are written the same way. Some might be fill in the blank, listing answers, or filling in a chart.

3.) ***Personal Study:*** These questions come from the book "Foundation of the Fire." They are meant for you to apply the answer personally or sometimes on a larger scale. The answers come from your own mindset so you can personally tap into what God desires of you.

4.) ***Activity:*** in this section, you will do something that relates to the chapter. This could be filling in a questionnaire, to getting outside items, or a challenge to do something for someone else. Each activity is meant to be fun, and give you the ability to remember the lesson.

5.) ***Personal Notes:*** the blank page at the end of every chapter is extra space for your notes. You can use this space for your notes while reading or answering the questions. Write scriptures for reference, use it for the activities, or use the section that will help in your study.

Table of Contents

Introduction

Please read Hebrews 12:25-29

"For our God is a consuming fire." Hebrews 12:29

"Foundation of the Fire," uses fire as a metaphor in building a strong relationship with Jesus Christ. We will study fire in various form and work: light, heat, melting, immersion, and energy to name a few. Studying fire gives us a recognizable symbol in remembering to anchor our foundation in God.

Hebrews 12:29 compares God as a consuming fire. What an interesting metaphor to compare God with this attribute of fire. Usually, we see God in the New Testament as a gracious and loving Being who died for our sins and became the light of the world.

Hebrews 12:25-28 refers to a time when God will move through the Earth and shake things up. The Lord will separate those who are for Him and those who are not. God desires to take His people home to Heaven, so a clear-cut separation between the two sides is necessary.

Hebrews 12:28 states, "Wherefore we receiving a kingdom which cannot be moved, let us have grace whereby we may serve God acceptably with reverence and godly fear." We cannot be moved from God or from what He wants us to be if we serve Him. Our lives must have reverence for God knowing that with Him in ultimate control, we can stand through hard trials.

Look closely to see in verse 26 it says, "Whose voice then shook the earth." God's Word will sweep across the land, touching people's lives to see if they will choose Him or the ideals of the world. The Lord is taking as long as possible so that all people will have a chance to meet Him in Glory. 2 Peter 3:9, "The Lord is not slack concerning His promise, as some men count slackness; but is longsuffering to us-ward, not willing that any should perish, but that all should come to repentance."

As of this moment, God is waiting and allowing us the opportunity to listen to His words. He wants you to build a firm foundation in Him so you can live eternally with Him in Heaven.

In Luke 6:46-47 Jesus says, "Why are you so polite with me, always saying 'Yes, sir,' and 'That's right sir,' but never doing a thing I tell you. These words I speak to you are not mere additions to your life, homeowner improvements to your standard of living. They are foundation words, words to build a life on." (The Message)

Jesus gives a parable about two types of people. Both groups claim the name of Jesus but only one has set up a true relationship with Him. The group who has a firm foundation in the Lord has three characteristics, which we ourselves can follow.

First, they come to God. This is important because they have to show the Lord they are serious by taking that first step. In our mindset, we have to desire to become what God wants us to be. It could be deciding to stop drinking if an alcoholic; never visit cities with huge gambling centers if addicted to gambling; to stop gossiping; or to open our Bible more often because it is collecting dust. Whatever the process is, the first step is to come to God. "Come unto me, all ye that labour and are heavy laden, and I will give you rest," Matthew 11:28. True peace will only come in our lives if we choose the Lord. Nothing on this planet can bring us satisfaction like God dwelling in our hearts.

God does not expect us to be perfect before coming to Him. Matthew 9:12-13 "But when Jesus heard that, He said unto them, They that be whole need not a physician, but they that are sick. But go ye and learn what that meaneth, I will have mercy, and not sacrifice: for I am not come to call the righteous, but sinners to repentance." The Lord has a yearning for us to come as we are. No matter what our weakness is, the Lord desires for us to come to Him. Believing that we can change without God is flawed thinking. God has all power to change us but only if we are willing to come and accept His modifications in our lives.

The second part is to listen to Jesus' words. Listening is important to building a relationship with God. "…He did this to make you understand that man does not live by bread alone. But man lives by everything that comes out of the mouth of the Lord," Deuteronomy 8:3 (NLV). We have to listen to what He is saying so we can build a relationship with God.

Gaining knowledge about Christ is important to our growth. The Lord has a wealth of information to give us for help. The Bible is the greatest source for learning Christ's words but not the only one. Other resources include songs, sermons, church services, people's lifestyles, books, dreams, and prayer. Regardless of the resource, listen to what God is communicating to build a stronger relationship with Him.

Lastly, after listening, do what Jesus says. "But be ye doers of the word, and not hearers only, deceiving your own selves," James 1:22. This means when God tells us to do something, do it. He is not speaking to hear Himself talk. God expects action to take place. God spoke and things were created (Genesis 1). There is power in the words of God. For us to resist the temptations of the world, we have to communicate with God daily and put His instructions for our lives into practice.

Jesus was informing the people what it takes to build a foundation with the Lord. Building a foundation in God will put you in His camp instead of the other. Jesus showed them the difference between the groups in a parable.

Luke 6:48-49 tells the account of two men who built their homes on two separate foundations. Both men have the same house and materials, but one builds it on a rock and the other in sand. Verses 48 and 49 begin by stating that both men have listened to the words of Christ. This means that both came to Christ and has access to the same scriptures and information to grow stronger in the Lord.

However, the difference is that the man who built His home on the rock was the man who did what Jesus says. "…when the flood arose, the stream beat vehemently upon that house, and could not shake it:" Luke 6:48. By doing what God says, the man was able to withstand the storms of life. Although wet, the home remained, and so it is with us when we build a relationship with God. Compare this to the man who did not listen to the words of God. "…is like a man that without a foundation built a house upon the earth; against which the stream did beat vehemently, and immediately it fell;" Luke 6:49.

We all have some type of access to the Bible, everyone can get some type of message from God, and all people will have a chance to be able to experience Jesus in some form or fashion in their lives. The true difference is what will be done when the knowledge is given. Listening is not enough, as shown in the parable. We must also obey. Jesus knows what is needed in our lives for us to withstand the world.

David in 2 Samuel 22:2 talks about being anchored to the rock, who is Jesus. "…The Lord is my rock and my fortress…" The same sentiment is understood in the new testament where

Paul writes, "And did all drink the same spiritual drink: for they drank of that spiritual Rock that followed them: and that Rock was Christ," 1 Corinthians 10:4.

Our foundation needs to be anchored in Jesus. Not only do we need to come to Christ and listen to His words, but also, we need to do His will. By completing all three steps, it digs us deeper into Jesus. This way when problems and trials come our way; we are able to stand and not be destroyed. The time will come for God to cause a separation between those who will go with Him and those who will not. Our foundation in Christ will make all the difference.

This book will give us a starting path to building a foundation with Christ. Albeit some of us have been in church all of our lives while others are picking the Bible up for the first time. We will delve into the Bible so you can have information for starting a relationship with Jesus. Building a foundation will bring peace like no other in this world, "Foundation of the Fire," is a starting point.

Quoted Scriptures

Hebrews 12:25-29 For Our God is a consuming fire
2 Peter 3:9 The Lord is not slack concerning His promise
Luke 6:46-47 They are foundation words, words to build a life on *(Message)*
Matthew 11:28 Come unto me, all ye that labor and are heavy laden
Matthew 9:12-13 For I am not come to call the righteous, but sinners to repentance
Deuteronomy 8:3 Man lives by everything that come out of the mouth of the Lord *(NLV)*
James 1:22 Be ye doers of the word
Luke 6:48-49 He is like a man which built an house, and dig deep
2 Samuel 22:2 The Lord is my rock
1 Corinthians 10:4 Drank of that Spiritual Rock…that Rock was Christ

Scripture for Future Study

Genesis 1 Creation account
Mark 5:1-20 Man healed when encountering Christ
Hebrews 12:25-29 God as a consuming fire

STUDY GUIDE

1.)   What element are we using to compare God?
FOTF Pg 7

2.)   Why is there a wait before the Lord returns?
2 Peter 3:9, FOTF Pg 8

3.)   All people must come as they are to the Lord. Matthew 11:28 refers to bringing your
        burdens to the Lord. List three burdens/problems that you want God to remove.

        A.) _____

        B.) _____

        C.) _____

4.)   Now that you have the three, describe how each effects your relationship with God and people.

      A.) with God   _____

          with people _____

      B.) with God   _____

          with people _____

      C.) with God   _____

          with people _____

5.)   The second part of Jesus lesson is to listen to His words. Read **Deuteronomy 8:1-3** and explain the importance of God's word.

6.)   How is faith and works connected?
James 1:18-26

7.)   Name one thing you can do to change the behavior/attitude toward each of the three problems you have written down from question 3. Remember that each of them can range from counseling, to having a friend give you help.

A.) _____

B.) _____

C.) _____

8.)   Christ uses a parable to compare two people who are building a relationship with Him. Describe this parable.
Luke 6:48-49, FOTF Pg 9

9.)   Hebrews 12 talks about a separation when some will follow God and others will not. What will make all the difference?
FOTF Pg 9

PERSONAL STUDY

1.)   In what ways have God set up a foundation in your life? Review your family, schooling, work, friends, or other areas to see how the Lord has used them to help you in your life.

2.)   Hebrews chapter 12 talked about separating people who choose God and those who do not. In our society, what ways can you see this separation evolve?

ACTIVITY

Get 2 pieces of paper, some dust/sand, a medium size rock, and a flat surface.

Take the two pieces of paper and write on both, "My Relationship with God is founded on…."

Then get the dust/sand, put it on one sheet and put the rock on the other.

Blow on both. Which one was able to move? Which material is everywhere?

Your breath represents trials and problems that will come. The only question is where do you want your foundation? In which case do you feel peace and security?

Personal Notes

Chapter 1
Knowledge of God part 1

Please read Exodus 2:11-25

"Who maketh His angels spirits; His ministers a flaming fire." Psalms 104:4

When Moses encountered God at the beginning of Exodus chapter 3, he had a job. It was the tedious work of sheepherding, but he still was working. Moses did not have the Divine concept that by being a sheepherder he was actually learning crucial lessons of patience and leadership. Those skills would be used to lead millions across the wilderness and into a land that God had promised to Abraham, (Genesis 13:14-18). During this time, Moses was gaining knowledge so he could be of service to God.

Right now God is working in us a particular skill that will be needed for the future. Albeit a mundane job, studying in school, or learning life through other means; God is working in us to develop the skills and talents He has given so we can be of service. Just like Moses, talents are given to all people for various reasons and we have to be patient to allow those gifts to grow and mature. God has not created us to be stagnant, or never use the abilities that He has given us.

In chapter 2 of Exodus, Moses had to flee Egypt because he killed an Egyptian, (Exodus 2:11-12). Moses thought that his people would accept the slaying because it had helped them. In reality, this incident caused friction between himself and his own people.

To get God's work accomplished, violence or other radical means are usually not the answer. Often we have a deep desire to do God's will because it's innate. The Lord put it there so our natural inclination is to work for Him. However, we do this by our own ways and how we believe the work should get accomplished. By doing this, we only set ourselves up for trouble and failure sometimes by alienating friends, family, and church members. Other times, we set ourselves in trouble and end up going to prison or being exiled from a certain community. Do not worry or feel like God is unable to save you. The Lord is always willing to use us regardless of our past.

Moses killed a man and God continued to use him. God can use all of us. He is working in our lives, to mold and get us into a situation that will best fit Him. The Lord will guide us through a period to spend personal time with Him.

Exodus 2:16-17 recalls when Moses saved Jethro's daughters from the shepherds who where trying to scare them away from the well. Moses fought off the shepherds and helped the seven women get water for their camels. Moses was on foot, fleeing persecution from Egypt, but took the time to help someone else.

In our lives while we are moving away from some problem, trial, or terrible situation we can still help others who are in need. God will place us in situations where we will relieve the pain of someone else. The Lord does not want us to wait for some miraculous time of peace and perfection to happen for us to help others. God desires for us to use what we have and He will make up the rest, (Acts 3:1-7). If the ability is not there to go to the coastal towns and help Hurricane victims, then send clothes, money, or food. Others cannot donate blood due to various health reasons so volunteer at the Red Cross to assist others. Some of us have experienced a loss in the family and can now help someone else deal with death in theirs.

Moses had to leave his comfort zone in Egypt and go to Midian for the Lord to communicate with him in a personal way. There are times in our lives where God remove us from our comfort zones. Sometimes God places us in a different city, job, or another church. In some cases, it means a financial situation or physical problem that might cause us to move closer to Him. Remember that it is nothing permanent. God does not take pleasure in afflicting pain in His servants. "For I have no pleasure in the death of him that dieth, saith the Lord God: wherefore turn yourselves, and live ye," Ezekiel 18:32. If Moses had built a close relationship with God and learned patience in Egypt, he could have stayed and led God's people out of bondage.

God is leading us into our current situation because it is what's best to build a closer relationship with Him. Learn now in the current situation so you do not have to go through unnecessary trials, tribulations, and struggles in the future. Remember that even if we do God's will and follow in His ways, the Devil is still going to attack us. We will not have absolute perfect days but if we follow Christ, He gives us the strength and wisdom to endure.

When Jethro's daughters returned quicker than normal, he was surprised and asked how that was possible, (Exodus 2:18-19). When his daughters responded that an Egyptian, Moses, helped them, then Jethro immediately wanted them to return and bring Moses to his home. When Moses was brought to Jethro's home, he gave him food, a job, shelter, and a wife.

Moses was not immediately rewarded for helping the seven women. He waited at the well, never knowing if he was truly going to be given something for his assistance. God led him, and that made all the difference. After all, Moses was homeless, did not have much on him, and was probably hungry. Nonetheless, he waited.

We cannot go around helping people and expecting things in return. Instead, help because someone is in need and you can provide his or her blessing. Bless someone because innately that is what God has placed in your heart to do at that time. Often times we look for ways of how blessing people can help us in the end. God would want us to do things because it shows how much we love one another and that we love Him. "By this shall all men know that ye are my disciples, if ye have love one to another," John 13:35.

Then God, as he did for Moses, will provide for all of your needs, (Matthew 6:19-34). Moses was in need of shelter, food, a job, and companionship. God provided these blessings because Moses helped others.

God desires for us to be well fed, to have a job, and to have companionship. He knows our needs and wants, concentrating on that gets us nowhere. Instead, God wants us to concentrate on building a relationship with Him and to go about doing what He has called us to do. By simply having a change of mind to serve, then all of our needs and some of our wants will be met.

Having a wife, at that time, was more of a want than a need for Moses. However, God gave him that as a bonus for what he did to help others. Gaining a spouse is a huge blessing in a person's life if you allow God to choose the spouse. Then you will reach the full understanding on what it means to be blessed in a marriage, (Proverbs 18:22, Ephesians 5:22-33).

While Moses was working as a shepherd, the king who wanted to kill Moses died, (Exodus 2:15, 23). The Pharaoh at the time represented a wall that was blocking Moses from being able to complete God's will. While the Lord is currently working within us, he also has His hand in other areas of our lives that we cannot see nor control. Had Moses tried to free the people early, that king would have killed him on the spot, or at least would have never let the Israelites leave.

God knew this, and continued to use this time to teach Moses valuable lessons that he would use later in life. God even kept the king alive long enough until He knew Moses was ready to lead the people. When God is ready to use you, the walls and blockers that will stop you from doing His work will be removed.

Psalms 27:2 says "When the wicked, even mine enemies and my foes, came upon me to eat up my flesh, they stumbled and fell." God is stronger then all attacks that enemies might have against you. "No weapon that is formed against thee shall prosper; and every tongue that shall rise against thee in judgment thou shalt condemn," Isaiah 54:17. No one or thing can stop you from completing God's work as long as the Lord is in control. Remember that He has spent too much time with us to allow any unnecessary harm to stop the completion of His will. All attacks against us and any walls set up to be a block will fail. With God in control, nothing, except ourselves, will stop us from accomplishing His goals.

God works on a specific time in which everything has to be ready at a certain moment. Galatians 4:3-5 states that, "That is how it was with us. We were like children ruled by the powers of this world. But when the time was right, God sent his Son, and a woman gave birth to him. His Son obeyed the law, so he could set us free from the Law, and we could become God's children," (CEV). This is referring to a spiritual bondage that Jesus came to free us from, if we choose Him. God has provided a way of getting out of bondage and being able to join Him in glory. We have to except Him and be free from the slavery of sin.

So it was for Moses and the children of Israel but they where under physical bondage. They wanted to leave persecution and called on God in Exodus 2:23-25 for relief. The Lord knew of their pain and started the next phase of his plan in Moses' life to be able to help his people.

When the time is right, God will begin his next phase for you. While He is molding you, God is sending knowledge about Himself to be useful for whomever you meet. For Moses it was the Israelites, for Jesus the World. The Lord could set you up in your community, job, the city, state, or providence in which you live in. It might have to be a continent or people over the internet. There is a wide variety of people that we can help, teach, and release them from their bondage. This bondage could be physical, financial, spiritual or a combination of problems. We have to allow God to have that encounter with us as He did with Moses at the burning bush.

Quoted Scriptures

Psalms 104:4 Who maketh his angels spirits; his ministers a flaming fire
Ezekiel 18:32 I have no pleasure in the death of him that dieth
John 13:35 By this shall all men know that ye are my disciples
Psalms 27:2 When the wicked, even mine enemies and my foes…they stumble and fell
Isaiah 54:17 No weapon that is formed against thee shall prosper
Galatians 4:3-5 When the time was right, God sent his Son *(CEV)*

Scripture for Future Study

Genesis 13:14-18 God promise Abram an heir
Exodus 2 Moses life and flight from Egypt
Proverbs 18:22 Blessing in marriage
Matthew 6:19-34 God will provide for your needs
Acts 3:1-7 Peter and John heals a crippled man
Ephesians 5:22-33 Marriage guidance

STUDY GUIDE

1.)   What was Moses' job and what did he learn from it?
FOTF Pg 18

2.)   Moses took it upon himself to do something for his people. What was it and describe
         the reaction they had?
Exodus 2:11-12, FOTF Pg 18

3.)   What is your job/school study currently? Please include your work, school, church,
         or extra-curricular activity.

4.)   List the skills you are currently doing for the answer in question 3.

5.)   Look over your skills. In what ways can they be useful to people? For Moses it was patience and leadership. What are your skills teaching you?

6.)   Read the paragraph that begins "In our lives while…" List three things that you can do currently to help someone else.
FOTF Pg 19

        A.) _____

        _____

        B.) _____

        _____

        C.) _____

        _____

7.)   List at least 3-5 of your needs below. Then read **Matthew 6:19-34.**

8.)   What should you concentrate on in life and what assurance do you have that God will take care of those needs?

9.)   Look at Moses, what were his needs, and what did the Lord do for him?
FOTF Pg 20-21

10.)   Read the following scripture, **Psalms 27:2** and **Isaiah 54:17**, what can you take from these promises? Knowing this about God are you confident in being the person He desires you to be?
FOTF Pg 21

PERSONAL STUDY

1.)   Like Moses, God moves his people in phases. What are possible changes that can happen in a person's life that will start them on the path that God has designed?

2.)   Jesus came to free us from Spiritual bondage. Moses was born to free the Israelites from a physical bondage. What bondage are you going through that you desire God to remove? What obstacles have you overcame to help others going through a similar situation?

ACTIVITY

Remember from the Introduction chapter of the workbook and the three burdens you had (question 3). Take out a sheet of paper and write them on it. Then write one more thing that is blocking you from being where God wants you to be.

Read Matthew 11:28 and pray that God would remove those things. Afterwards rip up the paper and flush it down the toilet. This symbolizes you seeing the problem leave and God flushing it away.

Do you feel better? Are you a little more relieved of seeing God work?

Read Exodus 14. It is an example of people seeing God wash away a burden/problem that was holding them back.

Personal Notes

Chapter 2
Knowledge of God part 2

Please read Exodus 3:1-6

"And the Angel of the Lord appeared unto him in a flame of fire out of the midst of a bush…" Exodus 3:2

The beginning of chapter 3 in the book of Exodus takes us to the personal meeting of God with Moses at the burning bush. God lead Moses from the brook, to the King's Palaces, to Midian, and now to this bush. Moses next job called for a personal encounter with God. The next phase in his life was about to proceed and God needed Moses' full attention.

As we mature in Christ, God will reveal Himself in a more personal way. Our progress in building a foundation with God will become stronger because we have spent time with Him. Reading a few verses in the Bible or spending a few minutes in prayer will cause us to move closer to Him. Then we all will have that burning bush experience. Not necessarily in the physical form, in that some plant life will be on fire for our enjoyment but, in that God will begin to speak with us on a higher level.

For Moses it was the mystical formation of a bush being on fire but not consumed. For us it could be in our minds, dreams, how we decipher God's Word. Sometimes it can come through strangers, songs, sermons, or thousands of other ways. The Lord will set up an encounter with us no different then Moses. Remember that the bush was on fire but it was not consumed. Exodus 3:2 states, "And the Angel of the Lord appeared unto him in a flame of fire out of the midst of a bush: and he looked, and behold, the bush burned with fire, and the bush was not consumed." God choose this because it revealed to Moses what the Lord will be in his life.

When God reveals Himself, the method is based on who He is to that group or individual. For the seven churches mentioned in Revelations, (Revelations 2-3), God is different depending on the church. This is because each church had a different set of problems and need. The Lord realizes our differences so He comes to us in a variety of forms.

To Moses, God came as one who will protect and guide him. For some it will be that God will bless us more so we can help a wider group of people. There are some who God will comfort and be love for them because of their duties. The rest might see God like Daniel and John through dreams because of what He has for them. Realize that God will reveal Himself the best possible way for everyone on a personal level. His plans have been laid out perfectly and the Lord knows how to reach us.

There are three points that we can take from the bush being on fire but not being consumed with our own lives and how God reveals Himself to us.

1) God will catch your attention. In this case, a bush on fire caught Moses attention. For many people that would have signified the time to run and run fast from a bush being on fire or it would have meant to gather some water and put it out before it catches the rest of the place on fire. This means that it would not have worked for everyone, but God has His way of catching every person's attention. He knows each individual's personality and the process to gain a positive response.

For some people it could be seeing a horrific car accident that leads them to wonder about their own mortality and they change their life completely to God. For some it is the words of a kind stranger or doctor. Various people have visions while others read a text from the Bible that is clearer to them now than ever before. Then again, some of us will have a mystical experience like a burning bush or something else extraordinary that is unexplainable so that we know it could only come from God. Whatever method God chooses, He will get our attention. God knows how to bring a person to Him so He can prepare us for that next stage in our lives.

2) God will reveal His powers. The Lord wants us to have no fear nor doubt that while we are out in the world doing His will that a supreme force is working with us. A bush on fire in that manner immediately showed Moses that something of a supreme nature is going on. This is no different from the type of power God displayed for the Israelites during the plagues

(Exodus 7:14 – 12:51), or for Job when God revealed to him how great His powers are, (Job 38-41).

Jesus will exhibit that He is all-powerful and this power is available for us. Remember that we are set up to help bring people out of bondage. Albeit physical, spiritual, financial, or even emotional, God has set us up to bring freedom to His lost sheep. Nevertheless, these people being in bondage means that a force does not want them to be free. No different than Moses having to go up against another Pharaoh who was set on keeping the Israelites as slaves, so will this force want to keep hold of the World in bondage.

God allows us to see His powers to strengthen and give us knowledge that we will be victorious in all struggles of life. The Lord can show us His power by someone being healed miraculously, we miss being in a car accident by seconds, money from nowhere helps us out with school or with bills, or we are older now yet we feel 10-30 years younger. God has a variety of ways to show his powers in our lives. Sometimes it is seeing the sunrise every day or waking up healthy, but even in those cases God is revealing Himself and His love.

3) God desires for us to be close to Him. A bush is a plant and is perfect fuel for fire. It is not like metal or glass, which take a huge amount of heat to burn, char, or melt. Plants, like people, gasoline, and other flammable materials are organic and actually feed fire. It's fuel, and in most cases consumed and destroyed. Yet, this bush was on fire but was not being consumed.

The Lord was revealing to Moses that the bush was deemed worthy to withstand the presence of God, very much as Moses was deemed worthy to be there in front of the Most High. In this case, the bush represented Moses and the fire, God.

We also represent the bush and God desires to be wrapped around us. By showing up in our lives, He is deeming us worthy to withstand His perfection and power. Just imagine that everywhere we go God is right there around us doing two things. He is lighting our path and offering up protection.

In Psalms 27:1-2 it talks of God lighting our path and our enemies all around us are destroyed. God revealed to Moses that He would light his path and protect him from all danger. The Lord will do the same for us. Places that we could not see will be revealed. Protection is granted from all danger because God will block all attempts from the enemy.

Having God in our lives is like having a force field, in that everywhere we go the supreme power of the Most High is there as a covering. People might try to talk about us, but those darts are eaten up by God's power. Financial and spiritual struggles may come our way, but those arrows are burned. Physical problems are hurled at us, but those bullets of life are disintegrated because Jesus is there.

The bush also symbolizes our relationship with God. The Lord is there to nurture us so we can grow to our full potential. Just as the fire protected the bush from all harm, so will God protect His people from harm. God was also revealing that we can be in the presence of the Most High and will not be destroyed. The Lord showed Moses that He is the life, light, and protection in the shepherd's life. God is doing the same for us.

God has constantly desired to be with His people, but the physical separation between Himself and His people did not end until Jesus died on the cross and that normal block was torn down, (Matthew 27:51, Mark 15:38, and Luke 23:45). The veil in the Most High Place which was up for our protection was ripped, God can show up in our lives freely and at all times.

God called Moses from the burning bush in Exodus 3:4. This is similar to the call that God made to Isaiah, (Isaiah 6:8), when he called the prophet to be a witness to the people. The Lord is calling us. He wants Christians to answer so that He can build a foundation with us and move us to the next phase of our lives. The mere fact that you are reading the Bible and gaining knowledge of Him right now means that just like Moses, you are moving towards Him.

The decision in life is to gain knowledge of God, not with mere words but with actions in a desire to learn and love Him. Know that while we are moving towards Him, God has constantly been making an effort for us on a personal level. Right now, He is calling us, and all we have to do is answer. As we begin to move closer to God, He wants no barriers to separate Him from us.

That is why in Exodus 3:5 it says, "'Don't come any closer,' God told him. 'Take off your shoes, for you are standing on holy ground,'" (NLT). God does not want our shoes to get in the way. Shoes at that time and now represented protection, transportation, and style.

God is our protection from all spiritual and physical dangers. God is our transportation because He desires to show us where to go. God is our style because He wants to clothe us with righteousness so we can be an example to others while we are on this earth.

While Moses is standing at the bush, God begins to tell Moses who He is and His plan for him. Jesus as of right now is doing the same. Thoughts and ideas begin to spring into your mind with words from the Most High on what you can do for God. They will seem natural and easy because God is working Himself in you.

The Lord has created each person to know who He is. By truly building a relationship with Him, it allows us to be a complete and whole person. God loves us and every day He desires that we work on our relationship with Him. He wants to travel with our families, be with us at home, at work, and anywhere else along our journey. The Lord is everywhere and desires to be that way with all people. Even if you were the only person in the world, God would forsake all just so He can be with you.

Right now God is calling you to have a relationship, your only response needs to be "Here I am," and God will do the rest.

Quoted Scriptures

Exodus 3:2 Angel of the Lord appeared unto him in a flame of fire
Exodus 3:5 Take off your shoes, for you are standing on holy ground *(Living)*

Scripture for Future Study

Exodus 3:1-6 Moses meets with God at the burning bush
Exodus 7:14 – 12:51 The ten plagues
Psalms 27:1-2 Our pathways being lit
Job 38 – 41 God informs Job of his power
Matthew 27:51 Veil is ripped
Mark 15:38 Veil is ripped
Luke 23:45 Veil is ripped
Revelations 2 – 3 Letter to the seven churches

STUDY GUIDE

1.)   Describe the meeting between God and Moses.
Exodus 3:1-6

2.)   God reveals Himself in a variety of ways depending on the person and group. For Moses it was in the form of a burning bush. In the book of Revelations God shows Himself in different forms. Look at Revelations chapters 2 and 3. Next to each church listed below, write how the author describes God to that particular church.

Ephesus   Revelation 2:1-7   _____
                                         _____

Smyrna   Revelation 2:8-11   _____
                                         _____

Pergamos   Revelation 2:12-17   _____
                                         _____

Thyatira   Revelation 2:18-29   _____
                                         _____

Sardis   Revelation 3:1-6   _____
                                         _____

Philadelphia   Revelation 3:7-13   _____
                                         _____

Laodicea   Revelation 3:14-22   _____
                                         _____

3.)   Why is the Lord different to each church? Now next to each church list the works of
       that particular church. Is there a connection between who God is compare to what
       they do?

Ephesus   Revelation 2:1-7   _____

                                         _____

                                         _____

Smyrna   Revelation 2:8-11   _____

                                         _____

                                         _____

Pergamos   Revelation 2:12-17   _____

                                         _____

                                         _____

Thyatira   Revelation 2:18-29   _____

                                         _____

                                         _____

Sardis   Revelation 3:1-6   _____

                                         _____

                                         _____

Philadelphia   Revelation 3:7-13   _____

                                         _____

                                         _____

Laodicea   Revelation 3:14-22   _____

                                         _____

                                         _____

4.)   Below are lessons that we can use when gaining knowledge about God.

A.) **FOTF Pg 31**; God will catch your attention.
What event has God used to get your attention to come to Him? Some examples include the birth of a child, sickness, a big blessing, or a catastrophic event.

B.) **FOTF Pg 31-32**; God will reveal His power.
For Moses this was the visual of seeing a bush on fire but not consumed. Name at least one way God has revealed His power to you? It can be spiritual, physical, emotional, or financial.

C.) **FOTF Pg 32**; God desires for us to be close to Him.
What ways can you feel the Lord interacting in you life? What can you do to get closer to Him?

5.)   The Lord desired that nothing would come between Him and Moses. Even Moses shoes had to be taken off (Exodus 3:5). In what way does the removal of shoes represent needs that can block us from building a relationship with God?

FOTF Pg 33

PERSONAL STUDY

1.)   What ways do God speak to people and how has God spoken or revealed Himself to you?

2.)   It took Moses forty years of being a shepherd to gain knowledge and build a relationship with God. Then he was able to be of use according to what God wanted him to do. What does the experience of Moses teach us about being patient and looking at our lives at this moment in time to build and foster a relationship with God?

ACTIVITY

Now is the time to start building some knowledge in God. In your Bible go the concordance and look up something you want to know. Alternatively, if you are near a computer with internet connection then go to www.biblesearch.com and type in a search word.

You can look up a topic that you have a desire to gain better understanding. Look up at least three different words and write them below. Write out the scripture that goes with that word as well as other references in the Bible that is notated. Often scripture is highlighted with letters or numbers, which notate other scripture references. Look those up as well and see how the various scriptures connect.

     1.)

     2.)

     3.)

Personal Notes

Chapter 3
Focus on God's Will

Please read Revelations 3:14-22

"I counsel thee to buy of me gold tried in the fire, that thou mayest be rich;"
Revelations 3:18

God describes the Laodicea church as lukewarm. The church takes the middle ground instead of standing for something. God is clear, make a choice. It is okay to be balanced but if there is a clear-cut way to follow either God or Satan then a decision must be given. This church looked for a middle ground.

Laodicea represents those who take on a spiritual laziness when it comes to God's word. They are fine in what they are doing and choose not to be diligent in building a relationship with God. This happens because the groups of people are self-sufficient and depend on themselves.

We believe we are rich when we depend on ourselves. Often, this refers to Earthly riches just like the Laodicea church. "I am rich, and increased with goods, and have need of nothing;" Revelations 3:17. This need of nothing includes Jesus trying to help and guide us. We believe that because we can take care of ourselves, that we have no need of the Savior. Because we are so self-sufficient, we believe we have no need for God.

Jesus spoke against such self-sufficiency in Matthew 6:19-20. "Lay not up for yourselves treasures upon earth, where moth and rust doth corrupt, and where thieves break through and steal: But lay up for yourselves treasures in Heaven, where neither moth nor rust doth corrupt, and where thieves do not break through nor steal." Our minds should be set on God and eternal matters like Heaven and salvation, not on how many cars, homes, or clothing we may have.

The Lord is not saying that we are not allowed to have nice things. Many scriptures talk about God blessing His people and desiring them to be an example for the world. The problem is not the money, clothes, house, or things of the earth, but the priority of desiring earthly things instead of God. It's ok to be blessed, but do not allow the blessing to out weigh God's will. Everything on Earth will be destroyed. We cannot take anything with us to death or into Heaven. All things on Earth will remain on Earth, which is why Christ desires us to stop putting our emphasis on temporary things.

The book of Revelations mentions what happens to people who believe that they are able to sustain themselves without the help of God. "…knowest not that thou art wretched, and miserable, and poor, and blind, and naked," Revelations 3:17. The Lord is warning His people of what happened when we do not rely on Him. We walk around in spiritual darkness never realizing that we are worse then the filthiest of rags that litter the gutters in the busiest cities.

When we are spiritually ill, the Lord does not have a true home in us. By deciding to rely on ourselves, we take on the five traits mentioned in Revelations 3:17.

1) We are wretched, meaning that we are no good to God or people. Our lives are all about us, and no one is benefiting from our selfishness, including ourselves. We must realize that we do not prepare our own Heaven. Only God can do that, and the only way in, is to depend and listen to Him. God desires for us to be in constant communication with Him.

2) By being miserable, we are uncomfortable, not at peace, and unhappy. We are unaware of our constant state of shame, and believe that the more money we have then the better off we will be. With more money, we can pay bills and buy expensive items, but not all people who have millions are at peace. Many have a yearning for something else. They feel incomplete and desire more, so they fill their lives with more earthly riches, instead of with Spiritual completeness.

3) Poor, in this context, refer to unproductive and barren. If we only think about ourselves and not doing God's will, then we are of no use to Him. We're roaming around believing we are doing well, but in reality, nothing productive is being displayed. 1 Corinthians 13:1-3 states that we have various gifts to help people, but without love, it is worthless. 1 John 4:8 "He who is not loving did not know God, because God is love," (YLT). Without God, having talents, financial gain, and helping people is worthless. Living eternally in Heaven is the goal not temporal things like obtaining money and earthly possessions. We believe that we are being productive, but to God we are tilling the land unsuccessfully like a hamster in a stationary wheel.

4) Walking around blind is another attribute we have when we choose to go our own way. God looks down on us and sees that we are in Spiritual darkness. He is our only source of light. We would never walk around freely without any guidance or help if we could not see seven inches in front of us. We would bring a map if we where traveling to an unknown area. Walking around this world, believing that we can do it on our own, is like going to an unknown area of the country without a map and hoping that the street we're on will take us to our destination.

5) The text refers to us being naked, meaning we are defenseless and unprotected. We walk around assuming that everything is okay, but without God, we do not have the spiritual protection to block us from evil, calamities, and problems. Life is ready to take us down; it is waiting for prime moments to harm us and we allow it access when we do not choose to follow God's plan. Imagine going to a battle and the only protection you have is your skin. No armor, no clothes, and no weapon. To most people this would be foolish and the warrior would die as soon as the enemy saw them. This is how God sees us when we decide to take matters into our own hands, foolish, because we are defenseless but believing that on our own without any Spiritual clothes, armor, and weapon, we can take on an enemy that is more powerful than we can imagine.

Sometimes we choose to be self-sufficient. At other times, our "luke-warmness" gets us to rely on ourselves. Not all people choose to deviate from God's plan. A level of comfort can be achieved on this planet, and this lures us into a sense of security in our own wealth and knowledge instead of trusting in God. In spite of the five attributes, God does not allow anyone to wallow in their own mess and not have a plan to fix their situation.

Acts 20:9-12 refers to an account where a man named Eutychus was listening to Paul preach at a house on the third floor. While there, he went to sleep in the window and fell to his death. The disciple calmly went downstairs and revived him back to life and Eutychus is forever known as "fortunate" because of what Paul was able to do for him.

Eutychus represents the people who are at church and fall asleep. Sometimes various matters in our lives become habitual. We should treat Spiritual matters with the same joy we had the first time we experienced the flavor. For example, communion can become mundane to some because of its consistency. It shows up like clockwork all the time so we take it for granted. Religious practices can be routine during worship, praise, Bible study, or other rituals. We forget that there is a relationship being nurtured with God every time we worship Him. We fall into a spiritual sleep and before we know it, might have fallen out of God's presence.

However, just as Eutychus was brought back to life, Jesus will do the same for us. God will not leave us out there to fall endlessly into a deep Spiritual sleep and have us to die in that condition. He is working constantly for our good to wake us up and continue a relationship with Him. God desires that all people wake up from Spiritual sleepiness.

Jesus is imploring us to rely on Him. He is sending out warnings so we can freely come to Him and realize that we are no better off now than the early Christians were when they were being persecuted. God desires us to be complete and out of spiritual darkness. Verse 17 in Revelations chapter 3 has the symptoms and problems with our current condition of not focusing our efforts on Him. Verse 18 has the cure.

"I counsel thee to buy of me gold tried in the fire, that thou mayest be rich; and white raiment, that thou mayest be clothed, and that their shame of the nakedness do not appear; and anoint thine eyes with eye salve, that thou mayest see," Revelations 3:18. God wants us to be better than the situation we are in right now. He knows of our troubles and our ways. Jesus sees us traversing through the halls of life in darkness and desires for us to get out. God has a process for us to focus on Him and not on ourselves.

God desires us to put on clothes of righteousness. He desires for us to be pure and protected. Whenever anyone desires to build a relationship with God, it brings you into the immediate battleground with the enemy. There is no middle ground. You are either with God or not and when you choose to be with God then the other side is desperately working to go against you.

When we put on the garment of righteousness, it is stating to the enemy that you are God's child and that you are under His seal and protection. A certain amount of peace comes from this because we are walking around knowing that we are protected and insured against all dangers. All of our faults and problems are covered up, so when people see us, they do not see our past. When new people see us, they do not see the effects of our struggles. All they see is God wrapping His robes and garments around His people, and to the Lord that is all that matters.

The Lord also desires to clear our eyes of sin and evil, and open them to His ways and path. Whenever we decide to be self-sufficient we are walking around in spiritual blindness, but God's cure is the moistening powers of the Holy Spirit. With the Spirit's direction, we begin to see clearly and walk more confidently because we can see the way.

"The Spirit of truth, is come, He will guide you into all truth: for He shall not speak of Himself; but whatsoever He shall hear, that shall He speak: and He will shew you things to come," John 16:13. The Holy Spirit is like a map and guide to your destination. No different from when we go on a trip we must look at that map to see where we started and where we are going. However, all of our faith and belief is that the map is correct and as long as we stay on the correct roads, according to the map, then we will arrive where we need to be. If our destination is hundreds or thousands of miles away, our eyes cannot see that far. We have to rely on the map to take us there and not our own sight.

The Holy Spirit is no different in that He will reveal to us how God was there in our past and the destination where He wants us to be. Our eyes, much like a vacation, cannot see that far into the future so we have to rely on Him for guidance. The Holy Spirit will lead us around any roadblocks, traffic jams, and other problems that will hinder us from getting to our destination. Each person's ultimate goal is Heaven, but how we get there is by the direction and control of the Spirit of Truth, which is the Holy Spirit.

By depending on the Spirit we began to see clearly now, and start to honestly walk in faith and not by our own sight. "For we walk by faith, not by sight," 2 Corinthians 5:7. God wants us to depend on Him because unlike us, He can see ahead and knows what is best for our travel. While on the road to eternal life, God has stops, rest areas, refilling stations, and all types of other means for us to be able to continue. The Holy Spirit is there to make sure we never get off path, or if we do, then He is right there to guide us back to where we need to be.

He wants us to buy gold tried in fire, which means that He has a purpose and plan for us. It is priceless and it deals with three sections of our lives. God wants His people to be physically, financially, and spiritually blessed, (3 John 1:2).

Matthew 6:33 states "But seek ye first the kingdom of God, and His righteousness; and all these things shall be added unto you." Our main goal is to seek out what the Lord has for us. God will take care of our needs as long as we focus on building a foundation in Him. God watches out for birds, plants, bacteria, and even forces such as wind and water; yet He did not die for any of them. Our pets, God loves them just as much as us, but He did not shed His blood for them. So if He is willing to make sure they are taken care of, how much more is He willing to make sure we are okay?

We focus on earthly things because that is what our senses tells us is real. It is too hard to believe that an omnipresent Being is up above mapping out our every move from now until He returns. God is right here making sure that the next few seconds is under His complete control. All the way until a month, a year, or even a decade from now, Jesus has each person life planned. He is here watching over us hoping that we will follow His way instead of our own. The Lord is in continuous interaction with everything around us, to make sure our lives are on track to meet Him in Heaven. God wants nothing else but the best for those who claim Him. We have to be willing to accept it.

Matthew 7:7-11 and Luke 11:11-13 teaches us to ask God for what we need and to seek it out in Him. By turning to Him, we are in constant interaction with the one true Being that can make all of our needs and wants come true.

God has setup "gold" which has been tried and formed just for us. This means that each person has their own individual blessing that was tailored especially for them. The right amount of impurities was removed and the weight is perfect. God made sure to polish it before giving it to us, so that it can be used in our lives. What the Lord has for each individual is amazing and more than we can ever imagine. He even counsels us to buy of this gold so we can be rich with peace and be blessed.

The Lord has given us the money or the means to be able to buy from Him the gold or His plans for us. In Isaiah 55:1, it states, "Wait and listen, everyone who is thirsty! Come to the waters; and he who has no money, come buy and eat," (AMP). The Lord desires us to come as we are. All we have to do is show up and have a desire to buy what God has promised. All He ever wanted was us. Our money, talents, and things are just mere actions of us showing what should be in us all along, love. God desires us to build a firm foundation of love in Him. By us showing up to buy, God is willing to give to us whatever we desire, because our desires will be changed to form what is needed not only for ourselves but everyone else around us.

God has made a promise to make us rich with peace in our lives. He wants us to be in complete harmony with Him knowing this is the best possible plan for everyone. The gold that He has promised His people is waiting for us to choose Him instead of relying on ourselves. Self-sufficiency might get us somewhere on Earth, but nowhere in Heaven.

The foundation that you build in God will lead to blessings that are more abundant then ever imagined. By ourselves, we are wretched, poor, naked, blind, and miserable; with God we are blessed, clothed and can see. If we saw two men, one who is self-sufficient, naked has no money, cannot see a thing, is not at peace, and is in pain; we would never choose to be that way. Compare that to the person, who is dressed in the best of clothing, can see perfectly, is at peace, and has the best of everything; everyone would want and desire to be like him.

This is how God looks at it. By building that strong foundation in Him, the difference is clear. That is why there is no lukewarm or middle ground. To God its simple, follow Me, and your life will be blessed more than you can even imagine. There are gifts and blessings that are untold waiting to be given if you will choose Him instead of yourself. It's tough to see how much better off we would be with Christ. Then again, it is tough to see anything in Spiritual darkness.

God is waiting on you to choose Him.

Quoted Scripture

Revelations 3:18 I counsel thee to buy of me gold tried in the fire, that thou mayest be rich
Revelations 3:17 I am rich, and increased with goods, and have need of nothing
Matthew 6:19-20 Lay up for yourselves treasures in Heaven
1 John 4:8 God is love *(YLT)*
John 16:13 The Spirit of truth, is come, He will guide you into all truth
2 Corinthians 5:7 For we walk by faith, not by sight
Matthew 6:33 Seek ye first the kingdom of God, and His righteousness
Isaiah 55:1 Wait and listen, everyone who is thirsty *(AMP)*

Scripture for Future Study

Matthew 7:7-11 Seek God for things
Luke 11:11-13 Seek God for things
Acts 20:9-12 Paul reviving Eutychus
1 Corinthians 13 Working with love in our hearts
3 John 1:2 Three areas of blessings in our lives

STUDY GUIDE

1.)   What does the Laodicea church represent?
FOTF Pg 43

2.)   When do we believe we're rich?
FOTF Pg 43

3.)   Is it wrong to have nice things? What is the true problem?
FOTF Pg 44

The biggest problem most people have is relying on self. Pride or a belief that you can do anything you want without God is the original sin. It still plagues our society and we actually lift one another up because of it. We have to remember that God should take the primary stronghold in our lives. If we remove God and replace it with ourselves then we are elevating our status above God.

4.)   Read the scriptures below. Then describe who is elevating themselves above God and why? Did it or will it work out for them because of what they wanted to do?

Genesis 3:1-19, Isaiah 14:12-23, Revelations 12:7-12, Revelations 20:1-10

5.)   Revelations give five traits of people who are self-reliant instead of relying on God. Write out what they are and give an example of how someone could show this behavior. **Revelations 3:17, FOTF pg 44-45**

A.) _____

_____

B.) _____

_____

C.) _____

_____

D.) _____

_____

E.) _____

_____

6.)   Not all people choose to be self-sufficient. What is another way that people can rely on self instead of God? How does this happen?
FOTF Pg 45

7.)   Who is Eutychus and what event happened to him? In what way have you been blessed like him?
Acts 20:9-12, FOTF Pg 45-46

8.)   God will not allow His people to wallow in this existence without offering help. What are three ways God to teach us to break the self-centered cycle and rely on Him.
Revelations 3:18, FOTF Pg 46-48

First Pg 46 _____

_____

Second Pg 47_____

_____

Third Pg 47-48 _____

_____

9.)   Notice that God's plan name three characteristics/behavior compare to the five of being selfish. God's ways are always easier and lighter when compare to doing it our way. Write out three things that you know would be easier if God was in control instead of self.
        A.)

        B.)

        C.)

10.)   Where should your focus be? What is God waiting on?
FOTF Pg 49

PERSONAL STUDY

1.)   What ways do we see the church of today as lukewarm? How should the church be in society and how can we be more like what God desires?

2.)   Why is it hard to focus on God's will for our lives? What can we do to make it easier to trust Him?

ACTIVITY

Remember how God wants you to rely on Him in this activity and we will act on these ways according to scripture. This way you can have a better memory of what was learned and apply it to your life.

First, write out the five ways a person can be self-sufficient. They are listed in Revelations 3:17 or question 5.

After this for the next three days when taking a shower/bath/getting clean, ask God to wash away all possible traits from your behavior or character. It's easy for us to think of random things while bathing, but ask God to keep you focus.

Then during the same three days, ask God to choose the outfit. Try not to fight Him and honestly put on what He desires you to put on. Remember that God wants you to look your best because you are representing Him, so He will not play jokester and make you look like an idiot. Trust Him.

Lastly during the same three days do at least one good deed for the day. It can be giving food to someone, going out of your way to help a co-worker, or speaking to people who you've never spoken to before. But each day, "buy" into being a representative of God and showing love to His people. You don't have to use money but use your talents, skill, and time to make an impact.

Over those three days, write out what you did and how you felt over each section.

At the end of the three days, get the sheet with the five self-relying characteristics and "X" out each one. Pray that God will remove these from you, rip up the paper and flush them down the toilet or remove it from your home. This is you seeing God take care of those inner problems and removing them from your life.

	DAY ONE	**DAY TWO**	**DAY THREE**
	Wash/Shower	Wash/Shower	Wash/Shower
What you did.			
How you felt.			

	DAY ONE	**DAY TWO**	**DAY THREE**
	Outfit	Outfit	Outfit
What you did.			
How you felt.			

	DAY ONE	**DAY TWO**	**DAY THREE**
	Good Deed	Good Deed	Good Deed
What you did.			
How you felt.			

Use this area to write out any details on a day to day basis as well as the total effect from this three day experience.

DAY ONE

DAY TWO

DAY THREE

TOTAL EXPERIENCE

Personal Notes

Chapter 4
Communicating with God

Please read Jeremiah 20:1-9

"But His Word was in mine heart as a burning fire shut up in my bones…" Jeremiah 20:9

After Jeremiah had proclaimed once again that Jerusalem and Judah will come under the power of an advancing army (Jeremiah 19), the High priest Pashur had Jeremiah beaten and thrown in prison, (Jeremiah 20:1-2). Jeremiah's proclamations were so Israel would change and become a symbol to lead other nations to God.

While Jeremiah was down in the prison, he was upset at God for being in jail and beaten. He believed whole-heartedly when God told him "Be not afraid of their faces: for I am with thee to deliver thee, saith the Lord," Jeremiah 1:8. When God was calling Jeremiah, He promised the prophet protection and courage. Jeremiah looked back at this and believed that something went wrong. In his complaint, he says, "You tricked me, Lord, and I was really fooled. You are stronger than I am, and you have defeated me. People never stop sneering and insulting me. You have let me announce only destruction and death. Your message has brought me nothing but insults," Jeremiah 20:7-8 (CEV).

The prophet who had spoken God's word, was confused, and believed that God had betrayed Him. The mere thought of the Most High sickened him and he called God a deceiver. The most infamous deceiver is Satan, whose very name means deceiver. This great man of God was now comparing God to the greatest enemy the universe has ever seen.

Being down is a part of life. We often look at ourselves and feel like God has left us, or has caused some great tragedy in our lives because we misunderstood His promises. God promised Jeremiah that He would deliver him from harm, but never completely keep him away from it. For most of Jeremiah's early years, he was kept from harm. Sometimes while doing God's work we take His protection for granted. We forget, it is God and not ourselves who is the ultimate protector and provider.

Jeremiah brought up two aspects for not wanting to do God's will. The first of which is in the mental realm. Verse eight of Jeremiah 20 states "because the Word of the Lord was made a reproach unto me, and a derision daily." Internally Jeremiah began to distaste the Word of God. He could not handle it and could only think of the problems and not God being in control.

We go through situations where we begin to look at things with our minds, which are muddy and sinful instead of through the mind of God, which is clear and perfect. The depression gets us down and the mere site of the Bible begins to put a mental bad taste in our heart. We do not want anything to do with the Gospel because it conjures up bad feelings of how we felt betrayed.

Then in verse nine Jeremiah said, "Then I said, I will not make mention of Him, nor speak any more in His name." This is the physical aspect of us saying that we will no longer represent God. Many people do this by choosing never to work in the church again, leaving the church, or becoming indifferent to God's words and His people. The act of helping someone out of love brings trouble to our hearts. We feel ill if someone mentions God in any way that is not bad or agrees our downtrodden state of mind.

Why bring this up? Because sometimes this is how we feel as we traverse on our road to building a relationship with the Lord. Troubles will come, and so will problems. Our attitude towards them will greatly affect how we begin to feel about God. If we are stuck in a bad mood then it begins to work on our mental state until we will no longer physically do anything for the Lord. However, if we decide not to stay in those negative moods, then we are open to God revealing His love toward us.

We go through death in the family, sickness, financial trouble, problematic children, and annoying people on your job, heavy schoolwork, church problems, and many other situations that cause us to wonder what the Lord is doing. We begin to question God no different than Job did when he was going through a mess of problems. Why does God allow doubting people to be written about in the Bible? Answer: it is natural to feel alone.

Jesus even went through loneliness while dying on the cross. When the weight of all sins from Adam to the future was laid upon Him, Jesus cried out "My God, My God, why hast thou forsaken me," Matthew 27:46 and Mark 15:34. Sin and problems of this earth cause a natural separation from us in the earthly realm to God in the Heavenly realm. Jesus Himself felt this separation and the mere thought of not being able to be in some type of communication with God the Father was so unbearable that he cried out. However, if we were to stop right there it would appear that Jesus was in a state of depression that He felt like God had betrayed Him.

Often times this is where we are stuck as well. We are upset at some situation, or disappointed, and stay that way towards God. If it's a catastrophe, we blame God. We even name the worst disasters "Acts of God." Earth is full of problems and strife that are unimaginable. Living here, compared to the universe, is no different from living in the worst possible neighborhood magnified by a million.

Nevertheless, just like Jeremiah, God is able to deliver us out of every situation. Jeremiah was beaten, and thrown into prison, but God brought him out, and Jeremiah continued to preach even more fervently. Joseph was thrown in prison and got out to be second in power only to the Pharaoh, (Genesis 41). Jesus died but rose from the dead. We all have gone through some trials and yet we are alive and have the ability to do more things that are amazing.

On the cross, Jesus did what all people should do when faced with adversity. Talk to God. Jeremiah did it by getting out his personal feelings that he could not go on without God. The Word of God when placed in our hearts will begin to override our sinful imaginations. Jesus was beaten, bruised, stabbed, spit on, jeered, and suffered various other physical and emotional torments. Yet, He began on the cross a word from the Bible. "My God, my God, why hast thou forsaken me?" is the first verse from Psalms 22. This Psalms starts with pain in going through trial and ends in the last few verses with praises from people being able to declare God across the world. Jesus died so that we could freely go and preach salvation to the world. His last few words while in agony were about how His death and pain on the cross will bring a start to the joy and happiness of us being able to spread His teachings across the world.

Using the Bible while in a struggle means that we are deciding to put God first and allow Him to take control of our feelings. Jesus began with a Biblical text, because it showed His close relationship to stay in constant communication with God the Father. This was our example for us to do the same with Jesus. When we are going through problems and cares of this world, our first thought should be to turn to Jesus and not handle it ourselves. Go to Him and open that communication line on a daily basis.

Going to the Word of God means, we desire to have the Lord dwelling inside of us. By communicating with the Lord constantly, people will find themselves like Jeremiah when after he proclaimed that he would never speak God's word again, "But His Word was in mine heart as a burning fire shut up in my bones, and I was weary with forbearing, and I could not stay," Jeremiah 20:9.

The prophet's constant talk with God was so deeply ingrained that even when he thought he could leave God alone; the reality was he could not. God was dwelling inside Jeremiah and he could not escape it. The Word of God gave him energy that he never thought he had.

Fire in many cases is harnessed and used as an energy source. We see that in ovens, burners in labs, candles, and even heat in car engines. Fire's combustive forces push things around which causes movement and action. We use this action sometimes to power other things or the thing that is currently producing the fire. For example, we take fire to wicks so we can shoot fireworks into the air for our pleasure. We also use fire and heat in car engines to move pistons so this will churn the car and its axel and tires for movement.

The Word of God is like fire because it gives us energy and is a source that pushes us to move. Jeremiah himself said that he could not stay, meaning that he could not be there in one place. He had to move, the desire to go out and speak God's word to the people was stronger than his mental desire to disclaim the Lord. It was greater than the very pain he was feeling from the lashes he got at the hands of the high priest.

Jeremiah only got this energy because he had to study and listen to the Most High. The prophet was in communication with God and this stored up energy source is what allowed him to withstand the natural desire to disclaim the Lord.

God uses His words as means to dwell with us no matter where we go. Jeremiah 31:33 goes into detail how God decided to be with humans on an intimate level. "But this shall be the covenant that I will make with the house of Israel; after those days, saith the Lord, I will put my law in their inward parts, and write it in their hearts; and will be their God, and they shall be my people."

The Lord wants to be with us on a very personal level. He has always had the desire to dwell amongst His people. In Exodus, God told Moses specifically how He would meet with His people. "And thou shalt put the mercy seat above upon the ark; and in the ark thou shalt put the testimony which I shall give thee. And there I will meet with thee, and I will commune with thee from above the mercy seat…," Exodus 25:21-22.

God dwells on Earth where His testimony is located, because His laws, His words, His testimony is what connects us to Heaven. The same laws and foundations found on Earth are founded in Heaven.

However, the Israelites during the reign of kings chose not to follow God's law and to do it their way. Hence, from then on God changed where the testimony will be, which was above the mercy seat and now into our hearts. God is writing His laws in us so that no matter where we go, He is always there. We will have a natural inclination to build a relationship with God instead of waiting for someone else to tell us. His word can be available to all people; it is our job to seek that, which is in His testimony so that we can have a stronger connection and communication with Him.

Our own relationships, albeit with our significant others, parents, co-workers, friends, or schoolmates all have one thing in common for growth, communication. By talking to one another, we build up a close tie to that person. Notice how you are closer to the people you talk with the most. Sometimes, as we get older there are people who were our friends but never as close as the ones you are currently talking to right now. That is why we change from having the longest conversation of the day with our parents, to our spouses and children. By communicating, we are building a bond with one another.

God is the same with us. He has made it even easier so we do not have to kill animals and have a priest talk for us to Him. Instead we can open up our Bible, pray, sing, worship, praise, or use various other ways of communicating with Him. It does not happen over night but daily. We have to communicate with God all the time so that our relationship with Him is growing stronger each day.

There are times, like in human relationships that certain troubles or joys can bring us closer together. For example, soldiers in a war always have a close bond because of the struggles they face together. A married couple going through a life-changing event can sometimes grow closer together. Friends who share a horrific experience or even classmates who study together for a final can find themselves instantly moving closer to one another in bigger steps than on the day-to-day grind. This was the case for Jesus when He took the step to bare our sins, and for Jeremiah who went from possibly giving up when adversity struck, to feeling as if he had to go out there and preach God's word.

Even though these events can happen, we still have to spend every day in some kind of communication with God. Think back to some of the friends from elementary school or even in high school. There are those you keep up with and others you hardly know about. Some we use to be close with but now we don't know where they live or if they are even alive. Over time, without any contact the bond you thought was so strong will disintegrate. This goes for all relationships. Married couples have to keep up a healthy dose of communication and interaction with one another or their union will fail. Parents and children must talk or their bond will soon go by the wayside. Friends, co-workers, and any other types of relationships will also fail without communication.

God's words are a source of wisdom, life, and prosperity. Hosea 4:6 states, "My people are destroyed for lack of knowledge." Without a true knowledge of God, we go by the wayside like the man who built his home on sand instead of the rock, (Luke 6:48-49).

Building a foundation in God is not just reading the Bible but consuming it. God desires for us to make the Bible personal. For example, we should insert ourselves in the parables that Christ speaks about in Matthew 13. When we are reading about Jesus dying on Calvary, do not think about the world only, concentrate that He died for your personal sins. The time you read about some of the great leaders like Moses, prophets like Elijah, and common people like Ruth, put yourself in their shoes. What lessons is the Word of God teaching you? Don't always think on a grand scale, like people in the Church need to have patience. That might be true, but look at it as I need to have patience when it deals with a specific area in my life. Begin to change the mindset so God can dwell in you. To look at the Bible as a general source for data is only the beginning. We must grow and be fed with a deeper knowledge and love of Jesus Christ.

"When I was a child, I spake as a child, I understood as a child, I thought as a child: but when I became a man, I put away childish things," 1 Corinthians 13:11. As we learn more about the Bible, we begin to mature and grow. God desires for our communication lines with Him to mature as well.

"Now everyone who lives on milk is inexperienced with the message about righteousness, because he is an infant. But solid food is for the mature-for those whose senses have been trained to distinguish between good and evil," Hebrews 5:13-14 (HCSB). God understands that starting our intake of the Bible is similar to milk. We have to take it slowly; our system cannot handle all of the deep-rooted vitamins and prophecies. However, as we get spiritually older we should go from milk to strong meat, making sure that we are getting the full slate of Biblical truths that are needed to survive in this world. Only by maturing to the strong meat of God's Word will we build a deeper foundation in Him.

The Lord desires to be in you to your very bone marrow. He is in the electrons and atoms that make up the cells in your body. God wants to complete you and make sure that you are the best possible person that He has made. So when you talk to Him, not only go over some of your major concerns, but talk to Him about joys. Converse to God about what outfit He wants you to wear tomorrow. If you are a sports fan, then talk to Him about your favorite team. If you like books, talk to God about that, or even a favorite show. Maybe you have a hobby; God is interested in talking to you about that as well. Whatever is important to you, Jesus has deemed it important to Him eons before. Hiding it does not stop God from knowing what's on your heart. He loves you and wants to love the complete you.

By communicating with God, you begin to build a deep foundation in Him. Whenever struggles and problems come your way, you can say that truly, the Word of God is like fire and you have to move on. Communicate with God today and everyday for the rest of your life. See the difference that harnessing that Divine energy can do for you.

Quoted Scripture

Jeremiah 20:9 But His Word was in mine heart as a burning fire shut up in my bones
Jeremiah 1:8 Be not afraid of their faces: for I am with thee to deliver thee
Jeremiah 20:7-8 You have let me announce only destruction and death (CEV)
Jeremiah 20:8 Because the Word of the Lord was made a reproach unto me
Jeremiah 20:9 I will not make mention of Him, nor speak any more in His name
Matthew 27:46 My God, My God, why hast thou forsaken me
Mark 15:34 My God, My God, why hast thou forsaken me
Psalms 22:1 My God, my God, why hast thou forsaken me
Jeremiah 20:9 I was weary with forbearing, and I could not stay
Jeremiah 31:33 I will put my law in their inward parts, and write it in their hearts
Exodus 25:21-22 I will commune with thee from above the mercy seat
Hosea 4:6 My people are destroyed for lack of knowledge
1 Corinthians 13:11 When I became a man, I put away childish things
Hebrews 5:13-14 Now everyone who lives on milk is inexperienced with the message

Scripture for Future Study

Genesis 41 Joseph was taken out of prison
Jeremiah 19 Jeremiah proclaim problems for Judah
Jeremiah 20:1-2 Jeremiah is locked in prison
Luke 6:48-49 The two different foundations a person builds their home

STUDY GUIDE

1.)   What message caused Jeremiah to be imprisoned? Who put him there and would this
       be strange if a similar situation happened now?
Jeremiah 19, 20:1-2, FOTF Pg 61

2.)   What did Jeremiah say to God after being imprisoned and beaten? What lesson can
       you take from being frustrated with a situation?
Jeremiah 20:7-8, FOTF Pg 61

3.)   Name at least one tragedy that we attribute to God?

4.)   Now write out what warnings was given to help prepare people from that tragedy.

5.)   When looking over you life in times of hardship, did God warn you of that trouble?

6.)   What two ways did Jeremiah decide not to represent God?
Jeremiah 20:8-9, FOTF Pg 62

7.)   Seem like it would be strange to have a portion in the Bible where someone would doubt God. Why would this be allowed in scripture?
FOTF Pg 62

8.)   What did Jesus say on the cross while dying on Calvary? When you're going through struggle, do you find comfort in knowing that Jesus has experienced the same problems of being alone with a problem as you?
Matthew 27:46, Mark 15:34, FOTF Pg 63

9.)   Name the Psalms that Christ was quoting on the cross.
FOTF Pg 63

10.)   Now read it and relate the Psalms in two ways.
        First, how could this apply to Christ's situation on the cross?

        Second, what can you take from this and apply it to your life?

11.)   Jeremiah states that the word of God was like fire in my bones. Explain this metaphor
        and what example could we use today?
FOTF Pg 64

12.)   Where does God dwell? What level of a relationship does God desire?
Exodus 25:21-22, FOTF Pg 64-65

13.)   Name the one thing all relationships/friendship have in common?
FOTF Pg 65

14.)   Name a few ways we can communicate with God?
FOTF Pg 65

15.)   What happens if the line of communication goes down? Do you notice a difference between people from your past and those in your present?
FOTF Pg 66

16.)   What does the Bible state can destroy us?
Hosea 4:6, FOTF Pg 66

17.)   How should we build a relationship with God? What examples are given and name
         at least one thing you can do to make your relationship stronger?
FOTF Pg 66

18.)   Anything that lives; matures and grows over time. The Bible uses the examples of a
         growing child and going from milk to meat as a means of showing spiritual growth.
         What is a viewpoint or activity that you did while you was younger that you no longer
         do at your current age? What cause the difference in behavior/viewpoint on life?
1 Corinthians 13:11, Hebrews 5:13-14

We often come to God for two reasons; forgiveness or wanting something. This is great, but imagine if someone you knew only came to you because they did you wrong and needed forgiveness. On the other hand, if they wanted you to give them something.

19.)   How would you feel about someone like that? Would you continue to be close to them? Is that really a relationship/friendship?

20.)   List three things that you like, hobbies, or your dreams. Now the next time you pray spend some time to work that in the prayer or when you're talking to yourself, include God on the conversation. He knows that what you're thinking is important. If it's a concern for you then it's a concern for Him.

        A.)

        B.)

        C.)

PERSONAL STUDY

1.)   What ways can we communicate with God? Why is this important?

2.)   When going through trials, Jesus and Jeremiah relied on the Word of God for comfort. Go through the Bible and find scriptures that you can relate to so it can bring comfort during hard times. Why is having the Bible important for overcoming problems in our lives?

ACTIVITY

This activity will cover how you communicate in seven different relationships. The categories are, Jesus, Spiritual, Intimate, Family, Friend, Co-worker/Schoolmate, Your Choice. Below please put a name to the following categories. These will be the people you use for the questions below. Jesus is one of the categories so you can compare how you communicate with God compare to your human relationships.

Intimate – This is about your intimate relationship, for example, your spouse, fiancé, a person you are dating. If there is no one, then pick your best friend.

_____

Family – Someone you consider family. Usually blood related but often you have people who are family and are not blood. So choose the closest person, as long as they do not fulfill the intimate category.

_____

Friend – Think of a best friend, unless you used them for the intimate category, then pick your next closest friend.

_____

Spiritual – This can be your Pastor, Deacon, church member, someone you go to for Spiritual guidance or need.

_____

Co-Worker/Classmate – This is someone on your job or a classmate if you're in school.

_____

Your Choice – Normally I would use self, so you can see if you're honest with your feelings, but here you can choose any person you want but clearly not anyone you've already chosen.

_____

Below will be a series of questions and a ranking system. This part will refer to your action in communicating with them. Ten means you do it often, Five would be occasion, where as zero means never.

1.)   You communicate with them daily.

Jesus	10	9	8	7	6	5	4	3	2	1	0
Intimate	10	9	8	7	6	5	4	3	2	1	0
Family	10	9	8	7	6	5	4	3	2	1	0
Friend	10	9	8	7	6	5	4	3	2	1	0
Spiritual	10	9	8	7	6	5	4	3	2	1	0
Co-worker/Classmate	10	9	8	7	6	5	4	3	2	1	0
Your Choice	10	9	8	7	6	5	4	3	2	1	0

2.)   Talk with them about your hobbies and your general interest.

Jesus	10	9	8	7	6	5	4	3	2	1	0
Intimate	10	9	8	7	6	5	4	3	2	1	0
Family	10	9	8	7	6	5	4	3	2	1	0
Friend	10	9	8	7	6	5	4	3	2	1	0
Spiritual	10	9	8	7	6	5	4	3	2	1	0
Co-worker/Classmate	10	9	8	7	6	5	4	3	2	1	0
Your Choice	10	9	8	7	6	5	4	3	2	1	0

3.)   You tell them your inner most secrets.

Jesus	10	9	8	7	6	5	4	3	2	1	0
Intimate	10	9	8	7	6	5	4	3	2	1	0
Family	10	9	8	7	6	5	4	3	2	1	0
Friend	10	9	8	7	6	5	4	3	2	1	0
Spiritual	10	9	8	7	6	5	4	3	2	1	0
Co-worker/Classmate	10	9	8	7	6	5	4	3	2	1	0
Your Choice	10	9	8	7	6	5	4	3	2	1	0

4.)   You tell them about good times and when something great has happened.

Jesus	10	9	8	7	6	5	4	3	2	1	0
Intimate	10	9	8	7	6	5	4	3	2	1	0
Family	10	9	8	7	6	5	4	3	2	1	0
Friend	10	9	8	7	6	5	4	3	2	1	0
Spiritual	10	9	8	7	6	5	4	3	2	1	0
Co-worker/Classmate	10	9	8	7	6	5	4	3	2	1	0
Your Choice	10	9	8	7	6	5	4	3	2	1	0

5.)   You tell them about bad times and when something awful has happened.

Jesus	10	9	8	7	6	5	4	3	2	1	0
Intimate	10	9	8	7	6	5	4	3	2	1	0
Family	10	9	8	7	6	5	4	3	2	1	0
Friend	10	9	8	7	6	5	4	3	2	1	0
Spiritual	10	9	8	7	6	5	4	3	2	1	0
Co-worker/Classmate	10	9	8	7	6	5	4	3	2	1	0
Your Choice	10	9	8	7	6	5	4	3	2	1	0

6.)   When I have done them wrong, I go back to apologize.

Jesus	10	9	8	7	6	5	4	3	2	1	0
Intimate	10	9	8	7	6	5	4	3	2	1	0
Family	10	9	8	7	6	5	4	3	2	1	0
Friend	10	9	8	7	6	5	4	3	2	1	0
Spiritual	10	9	8	7	6	5	4	3	2	1	0
Co-worker/Classmate	10	9	8	7	6	5	4	3	2	1	0
Your Choice	10	9	8	7	6	5	4	3	2	1	0

7.)   You ask them for help.

Jesus	10	9	8	7	6	5	4	3	2	1	0
Intimate	10	9	8	7	6	5	4	3	2	1	0
Family	10	9	8	7	6	5	4	3	2	1	0
Friend	10	9	8	7	6	5	4	3	2	1	0
Spiritual	10	9	8	7	6	5	4	3	2	1	0
Co-worker/Classmate	10	9	8	7	6	5	4	3	2	1	0
Your Choice	10	9	8	7	6	5	4	3	2	1	0

8.)   Go out or do something with them (for Jesus, going to church, concert, nature walk, etc)

Jesus	10	9	8	7	6	5	4	3	2	1	0
Intimate	10	9	8	7	6	5	4	3	2	1	0
Family	10	9	8	7	6	5	4	3	2	1	0
Friend	10	9	8	7	6	5	4	3	2	1	0
Spiritual	10	9	8	7	6	5	4	3	2	1	0
Co-worker/Classmate	10	9	8	7	6	5	4	3	2	1	0
Your Choice	10	9	8	7	6	5	4	3	2	1	0

9.)   Make plans to go see them or talk with them.

Jesus	10	9	8	7	6	5	4	3	2	1	0
Intimate	10	9	8	7	6	5	4	3	2	1	0
Family	10	9	8	7	6	5	4	3	2	1	0
Friend	10	9	8	7	6	5	4	3	2	1	0
Spiritual	10	9	8	7	6	5	4	3	2	1	0
Co-worker/Classmate	10	9	8	7	6	5	4	3	2	1	0
Your Choice	10	9	8	7	6	5	4	3	2	1	0

10.)   I would like others to meet this person.

Jesus	10	9	8	7	6	5	4	3	2	1	0
Intimate	10	9	8	7	6	5	4	3	2	1	0
Family	10	9	8	7	6	5	4	3	2	1	0
Friend	10	9	8	7	6	5	4	3	2	1	0
Spiritual	10	9	8	7	6	5	4	3	2	1	0
Co-worker/Classmate	10	9	8	7	6	5	4	3	2	1	0
Your Choice	10	9	8	7	6	5	4	3	2	1	0

For the next set of questions, think about how you enjoy communicating in these relationships. Ten would mean very much, five would equal average, and zero not at all.

11.)   They know who I truly am.

Jesus	10	9	8	7	6	5	4	3	2	1	0
Intimate	10	9	8	7	6	5	4	3	2	1	0
Family	10	9	8	7	6	5	4	3	2	1	0
Friend	10	9	8	7	6	5	4	3	2	1	0
Spiritual	10	9	8	7	6	5	4	3	2	1	0
Co-worker/Classmate	10	9	8	7	6	5	4	3	2	1	0
Your Choice	10	9	8	7	6	5	4	3	2	1	0

12.)   I can be myself around them.

Jesus	10	9	8	7	6	5	4	3	2	1	0
Intimate	10	9	8	7	6	5	4	3	2	1	0
Family	10	9	8	7	6	5	4	3	2	1	0
Friend	10	9	8	7	6	5	4	3	2	1	0
Spiritual	10	9	8	7	6	5	4	3	2	1	0
Co-worker/Classmate	10	9	8	7	6	5	4	3	2	1	0
Your Choice	10	9	8	7	6	5	4	3	2	1	0

13.)   If they need me, I would be there for them.

Jesus	10	9	8	7	6	5	4	3	2	1	0
Intimate	10	9	8	7	6	5	4	3	2	1	0
Family	10	9	8	7	6	5	4	3	2	1	0
Friend	10	9	8	7	6	5	4	3	2	1	0
Spiritual	10	9	8	7	6	5	4	3	2	1	0
Co-worker/Classmate	10	9	8	7	6	5	4	3	2	1	0
Your Choice	10	9	8	7	6	5	4	3	2	1	0

14.)   Even in bad times, I will still communicate with them.

Jesus	10	9	8	7	6	5	4	3	2	1	0
Intimate	10	9	8	7	6	5	4	3	2	1	0
Family	10	9	8	7	6	5	4	3	2	1	0
Friend	10	9	8	7	6	5	4	3	2	1	0
Spiritual	10	9	8	7	6	5	4	3	2	1	0
Co-worker/Classmate	10	9	8	7	6	5	4	3	2	1	0
Your Choice	10	9	8	7	6	5	4	3	2	1	0

15.)   I want to try something new with them.

Jesus	10	9	8	7	6	5	4	3	2	1	0
Intimate	10	9	8	7	6	5	4	3	2	1	0
Family	10	9	8	7	6	5	4	3	2	1	0
Friend	10	9	8	7	6	5	4	3	2	1	0
Spiritual	10	9	8	7	6	5	4	3	2	1	0
Co-worker/Classmate	10	9	8	7	6	5	4	3	2	1	0
Your Choice	10	9	8	7	6	5	4	3	2	1	0

16.)   I'm learning new things about them.

Jesus	10	9	8	7	6	5	4	3	2	1	0
Intimate	10	9	8	7	6	5	4	3	2	1	0
Family	10	9	8	7	6	5	4	3	2	1	0
Friend	10	9	8	7	6	5	4	3	2	1	0
Spiritual	10	9	8	7	6	5	4	3	2	1	0
Co-worker/Classmate	10	9	8	7	6	5	4	3	2	1	0
Your Choice	10	9	8	7	6	5	4	3	2	1	0

17.)   I look forward to being around them.

Jesus	10	9	8	7	6	5	4	3	2	1	0
Intimate	10	9	8	7	6	5	4	3	2	1	0
Family	10	9	8	7	6	5	4	3	2	1	0
Friend	10	9	8	7	6	5	4	3	2	1	0
Spiritual	10	9	8	7	6	5	4	3	2	1	0
Co-worker/Classmate	10	9	8	7	6	5	4	3	2	1	0
Your Choice	10	9	8	7	6	5	4	3	2	1	0

18.)   I enjoy spending time with them.

Jesus	10	9	8	7	6	5	4	3	2	1	0
Intimate	10	9	8	7	6	5	4	3	2	1	0
Family	10	9	8	7	6	5	4	3	2	1	0
Friend	10	9	8	7	6	5	4	3	2	1	0
Spiritual	10	9	8	7	6	5	4	3	2	1	0
Co-worker/Classmate	10	9	8	7	6	5	4	3	2	1	0
Your Choice	10	9	8	7	6	5	4	3	2	1	0

19.)   I enjoy communicating with them.

Jesus	10	9	8	7	6	5	4	3	2	1	0
Intimate	10	9	8	7	6	5	4	3	2	1	0
Family	10	9	8	7	6	5	4	3	2	1	0
Friend	10	9	8	7	6	5	4	3	2	1	0
Spiritual	10	9	8	7	6	5	4	3	2	1	0
Co-worker/Classmate	10	9	8	7	6	5	4	3	2	1	0
Your Choice	10	9	8	7	6	5	4	3	2	1	0

20.)   Our relationship is healthy and growing.

Jesus	10	9	8	7	6	5	4	3	2	1	0
Intimate	10	9	8	7	6	5	4	3	2	1	0
Family	10	9	8	7	6	5	4	3	2	1	0
Friend	10	9	8	7	6	5	4	3	2	1	0
Spiritual	10	9	8	7	6	5	4	3	2	1	0
Co-worker/Classmate	10	9	8	7	6	5	4	3	2	1	0
Your Choice	10	9	8	7	6	5	4	3	2	1	0

Now add up the scores to see where your relationship stands with each person. Of course, these twenty questions don't reveal all about your relationships but it is a start. Compare the numbers and see who you are spending time and communicating with. Also, look at individual questions and see if the correct person is getting the attention, they deserve.

Person	Scores Ques 1 -10	Scores Ques 11 -20	Total
Jesus			
Intimate			
Family			
Friend			
Spiritual			
Co-worker/Classmate			
Your Choice			

Personal Notes

Chapter 5
Preparation part 1

Please read Malachi 2:17 and Romans 1:21-32

"For if we sin wilfully after that we have received the knowledge of truth, there remaineth no more sacrifice for sins, but a certain fearful looking for of judgment and fiery indignation, which shall devour the adversaries." Hebrews 10:26-27

There is a popular quote, "God knows my heart", and it is usually followed up with some kind of action that God would never ordain. God has clearly written in the Bible that if something is wrong, people should not say that it is okay. This is not what God had in mind. There is grace, mercy, but to purposefully go out and do something that is against God's will, and to say that the Lord is okay with it will lead to failure and pain.

"Ye have wearied the Lord with your words. Yet ye say, Wherein have we wearied Him? When ye say, Every one that doeth evil is good in the sight of the Lord...," Malachi 2:17. Doing wrong is not okay or good in the sight of the Lord. God is very clear with many of His judgments and laws, breaking them means we are separating ourselves from the Most High. In the book of Isaiah, God states how it is wrong to willfully do bad and convince ourselves that God told us to do it. "Woe unto them that call evil good, and good evil: that put darkness for light and light for darkness; that put bitter for sweet and sweet for bitter," Isaiah 5:20. There are three ways that we promote this flawed thinking about God.

1.) When we say that God is fine with evil. Sometimes while we are describing a situation or a solution that we came up with, we interject that God okayed our reasoning that was never meant to be. For example, a person stating that they had sex before marriage and God is okay with it because they are in love. You might be in love but God is very clear on not having sex before marriage, (1 Corinthians 6:18-19, 1 Thessalonians 4:3). Believing the Lord is okay with evil, promotes lies and heresies about God, then these people tell others until many are erring in their ways because of what was said.

2.) Sometimes, we see evil as being good, for example, beating someone to death because they angered us. It could be sleeping with someone who is not our spouse to make a child and promising to dedicate that child to the Lord. Defaming someone's character so they will not get a job we believe the Lord has promised to us.

These are a few examples of seeing the darkness as light. Its one thing to have the light in the midst of darkness, but another to believe the darkness is the light. This world is full of sin and pain, and Jesus has allowed a way for all those who come to Him to be able to see their way through life. To believe that the darkness itself is light means we are not seeing clearly. To do something wrong on purpose because we believe there is good in it, does not flow with God. He does not desire us to do evil for good. We may not be able to see God's plans or the methods He is choosing but it is still best to follow Him.

Moses believed that he would help his people out of slavery by slaying an Egyptian. The only thing that got him was 40 years of exile. It was not until Moses used God's plan that the Israelites could leave bondage. They left due to plagues, so the Egyptians would have a greater concept of who God is not how strong Moses was.

3.) The last means that Isaiah brings up about our faulty thinking is in the form of internalizing it. When it refers to "that put bitter for sweet, and sweet for bitter," Isaiah 5:20, it means we have to take the thought and knowledge of evil and make it a part of our lives. For us to taste food means we are consuming it, and the food is affecting our bodies and running through our system. It breaks down and becomes energy, vitamins, minerals, and even waste. Imagine if every time we ate something, our bodies would hold on to the waste and let go of the things we really need, it sounds backwards and disgusting. Now visualize a person saying that God understands that is how they work, and their bodies continued to hold on to the waste products and let go of the minerals and vitamins. That person would die and we would be standing at their gravesite confused. Why would a person do something so backwards and then say that God wanted them to do that?

This is how God looks at us when we take certain beliefs and go about internalizing and believing that we are correct. We substitute what is good for what is wrong and believe that it will make us ok. However, to the Lord this will only lead to our destruction. He desires to take us away from such thoughts so that we do not have to live and wallow in our own filth.

"Because, having known God they did not glorify [Him] as God, nor gave thanks, but were made vain in their reasonings, and their unintelligent heart was darkened, professing to be wise, they where made fools, and changed the glory of the incorruptible God into the likeness of an image of corruptible man, and of fowls, and of quadrupeds, and of reptiles," Romans 1:21-23.

When we say that God is ok with evil for our purposes, then we are bringing His character down to our level. The Lord is clear in that this is foolish thinking and not to be had by people professing to love the Lord. We do not realize it, but as we continue to do that which is wrong, we're moving to death and further away from life.

God desires for us to be made whole and to get us out of habits and temptations. He does not want us to stay in them and to believe that He is the reason why we are there. God can help, but we have to have a willing mind to accept it and the knowledge that if we are in trouble we need to call on Him. He does not want us to have a reprobate mind like the one Paul describes in Romans.

Romans 1:28 states that, "And even as they did not like to retain God in their knowledge, God gave them over to a reprobate mind, to do those things which are not convenient." While in the act, we cannot possibly say that God is okay with evil because we know it is wrong. Often times when people are faced with something that inside they know is not of God, they immediately put on a defense and then attack the other person for calling them out on it. The only way they believe that they are okay is by saying that God okayed it or that they cannot help themselves.

Verses 29-31 of Romans chapter 1 lists various evils that people have committed or done. It lists sex and murder right along side with backbiting and pride. To God it is all the same. Only in human understanding do we put more emphasis on one type of evil over another.

The result, "Who knowing the judgment of God, that they which commit such things are worthy of death, not only do the same, but have pleasure in them that do them," Romans 1:32.

Deep down inside, all people have certain faults that we're dealing with. It is our nature and the adverse affect of being born in this world. "Behold, I was shapen in iniquity; and in sin did my mother conceive me," Psalms 51:5. All of us have a weakness that will cause us to come to Christ for strength. Throughout the Bible, various people had their problems. For

Abraham it was faith; for Moses it was anger; David loved too many women; Thomas had a doubtful heart; and we can go on and on about various others. However, God used every single one. Each person had their problems and had they wallowed in it, would have died without hope of meeting Christ in Heaven, however, Jesus had other plans.

"For the wages of sin is death; but the gift of God is eternal life through Jesus Christ our Lord," Romans 6:23. Yes, to dwell in sin will lead us to death, but by turning to Jesus, we can then live. God desires us to live with Him in harmony and in peace.

When in Heaven there will be no more problems, financial struggles, sickness, seeing people you love die, worrying about your children, heartache from broken relationships, and many other problems that you are encountering. God desires to end all of that, but you have to come to Him honestly, so He can work on your heart. No matter the problems and sins that you are struggling with, God is more than able to remove those obstacles.

God has to prepare our minds to be ready to accept His teachings and words. None of us can substitute our methods just because it makes us feel good. The Lord has laws and standards out of love, not punishment. The more you turn to Him and look for His wisdom, the more peace you will have on this Earth.

Quoted Scripture

Hebrews 10:26-27 For if we sin willfully after that we have received the knowledge of truth
Malachi 2:17 Every one that doeth evil is good in the sight of the Lord
Isaiah 5:20 Woe unto them that call evil good, and good evil
Romans 1:21-23 Having known God they did not glorify [Him] as God
Romans 1:28 God gave them over to a reprobate mind
Romans 1:32 That they which commit such things are worthy of death
Psalms 51:5 Behold, I was shapen in iniquity; and in sin did my mother conceive me
Romans 6:23 For the wages of sin is death

Scripture for Future Study

Romans 1:21-32 Committing sins on purpose and going into a reprobate mind
1 Corinthians 6:18-19 Flee fornication
1 Thessalonians 4:3 Clear against fornication

STUDY GUIDE

1.)   Is it okay to believe that we can do whatever we want? Where will this type of behavior lead?
FOTF Pg 85

2.)   According to Isaiah what are three ways that we can willfully sin? Next to each come up with an example that fits.
Isaiah 5:20

        A.) Pg. 86

        B.) Pg. 86

        C.) Pg. 86-87

3.)   When we willfully sin what does this say about our relationship with God? What do
        we turn God into?
Romans 1:21-23, FOTF Pg 87

4.)   What does the Lord desire?
FOTF Pg 87

5.)   What is reprobate mind?
Romans 1:28, FOTF Pg 87

6.)   What is the ultimate punishment for those in reprobate mind?
Romans 1:32, FOTF Pg 87

7.)   Is it possible to be in reprobate mind and not even know it? How can a person go that
        far from the Lord?

8.)   What does God desire to do? What are we not suppose to do?
FOTF Pg 88

PERSONAL STUDY

1.)   Why do people make excuses or say that God is ok when they do wrong? How can this train of thought cause us to be separated from God?

2.)   In Romans 6:23 it states "For the wages of sin is death; but the gift of God is eternal life through Jesus Christ our Lord."

a.)   When we see the word wage, what does this mean and how does this inform us that sin is not accidental?

b.)   Because God has prepared eternal life through Jesus, does this mean that we can behave and do anything we desire? What does the second half of this text means?

ACTIVITY

For the next two days test to see if you willfully sin or do wrong. Reread Romans 1:21-32. Remember that everything from gossiping to witchcraft is listed.

Now pull out a sheet and title it "Willful Sins". Make sure that no one sees this, because it's between you and the Lord.

Make three columns and list them as verbal, action, and think. Then whenever you do something that fits in one of these categories make a slash in the correct column. Review the sheet and see what has the most slashes. Is there a section that is more then the others.

Do you believe that you where on good behavior because you knew you was taking an account for your sins.

Know that this isn't meant to bring you down but to reveal to you what God always knows. We're not perfect and if we could see that side of us constantly then maybe we would make a better effort to change.

Personal Notes

Chapter 6
Preparation part 2

Please read Malachi 3:1-3

"For He is like a refiner's fire, and like fullers' soap." Malachi 3:2

Malachi 3:1-3 refers to when God will send His messenger to the world to clean it up. This is referring to when John the Baptist went into the world to prepare the way for Christ, (Matthew 3:11). The world at that time needed to hear these words so the people would be prepared for Jesus coming. John the Baptist's words were like fire to the souls in that it began to prick at their hearts and make them realize that they need to get themselves ready for Christ coming.

Now Jesus has come and left, but will return, and once again Jesus desire this world to be ready for His soon return. Once again, like the past, Jesus is preparing people to go out into the world and speak the word of God like a refiner's fire. God is preparing the world and He desires to clean the hearts of people so they can accurately choose whether they want Him in their lives.

No different from the process of refining gold and silver, God is currently working on us in our lives. There are impurities and sin in our lives that God is desperately trying to remove if we allow Him to do so. Just like the process of refining gold, the process can be hot and bothersome.

We might go through pain but it helps develop our character and build a closer walk with Jesus. Joseph had been imprisoned not once, but twice. Genesis 37:20-27 retells the account where his own family imprisoned him and Genesis 39:19-23 recalls the Egyptians' placing him in prison. On both accounts, someone could have killed him right then, but God had mercy on Joseph so that he would not see death. For Joseph this was a struggle, but it helped him build a tighter relationship with God and took out the pride that he had when talking with people. His brothers' biggest problem was how their dad loved him and how Joseph would flaunt his dreams and higher standing in front of them. Granted, Joseph was not trying to be pompous but how it came across to his brethren was not useful to God.

The Lord then had to get Joseph into an uncomfortable situation where his talents and abilities could be used. Even a person who could interpret dreams could not imagine his road in life would go from the favorite son, to imprisonment, to being a top slave, to imprisonment again, to become the second highest man in the land of Egypt.

However, the Lord had to burn off some of the impurities in Joseph's character and place him where he needed to be. Just like a silversmith who watches silver carefully to know when it's ready, so does God while looking over our lives. He is burning off the impurities in our character and is molding us to be the greatest servants for Him. Jesus knows where people will be the happiest in their lives.

Our job is to make sure that we allow God total access to our mind. We need Him to be able to clean out the muck and mire of sin from this world so we can go about, and live the life He would want us to live. By stating that God wants me to do evil, puts up a block. It hinders the Lord from allowing a change to happen in our lives.

God looks at us as the most valuable things on Earth. He compares us to gold and silver, because we are precious in His sight. He desires for us to shine like gold and silver and be pure and worth more value to the world and Himself.

Not only will God purify us but also he wants to clean us. In Malachi 3:2, it refers to us going through a cleaning process with fuller's soap, or a launders' soap. Even now as we clean our clothes, we use special soaps to make sure the dirt and grime is taken away without damage and fading our garments. We take these outfits and they smell fresh and clean but we still have to dry them out so they can be ready for wear.

God desires to clean us and make sure there is no damage or fade in our character and lives. He desires for us to be ready for Him. The gold and silver resembles to the internal change that God will bring about in us, but the soap is about the external. Our look will be changed, our diet modified, and the way we act will be transformed. All of a sudden when people see us, they do not see the evil or the stains of trials and mess from tribulations. They see the good, clean, and pure ways of our new lifestyle. An outfit that is seven years old will look brand new on us, because God is shining through. Our car will appear fresh off the lot, even after a rainstorm, because God is in the vehicle. Our words will become like honey as it spread throughout the masses, while our love and actions are more desired than plants need the sun.

Why would the Lord do all this in us?

Jesus desires to get you prepared for His soon return, (Matthew 28:18-20, Mark 16:15, Luke 24:47, John 21:21-23, and Acts 1:9-11). He wants us to be ready and while this is happening, He is preparing us to get others ready. Much like John the Baptist who had to go through his own process of getting ready, so do we. Just like him, we have certain missions and goals that God wants us to accomplish. We do not have to be perfect, but willing to grow in Him so our lives will forever be maturing and molding to the character that He desires for us to be.

God is preparing you to be greater than you can imagine, in Heaven and in this world. You just have to let Him take over and prepare you for the service that you can give lovingly for Him and all people.

Quoted Scripture

Malachi 3:2 For He is like a refiner's fire, and like fullers' soap

Scripture for Future Study

Genesis 37:20-27 Joseph in the pit
Genesis 39:19-23 Joseph in prison
Malachi 3:1-3 A message to warn people
Matthew 3:11 John the Baptist is called to preach
Matthew 28:18-20 Jesus tells disciples of His soon return
Mark 16:15 Jesus tells disciples of His soon return
Luke 24:47 Jesus tells disciples of His soon return
John 21:21-23 Jesus tells disciples of His soon return
Acts 1:9-11 Jesus tells disciples of His soon return

STUDY GUIDE

1.)   What is the purpose of the message found in Malachi 3?
Malachi 3:1-3, FOTF Pg 96

2.)   Is our call similar for the current time?

3.)   What is God trying to do in our lives?
FOTF Pg 96-97

4.)   What did Joseph have to go through and why was the Lord allowing him to experience such hard trials?

FOTF Pg 97

5.)   Not only does the Lord want to purify us but He desires to do something else. What is it and what are examples of Him doing this?

FOTF Pg 97

6.)   What is God's purpose in purifying and cleaning our spirit and who we are?

FOTF Pg 98

PERSONAL STUDY

1.)   God prepares our character and behavior to be what He desires them to be. Like Joseph, who endured behavior modification while in prison, what changes in your behavior should the Lord change?

2.)   Why is our character important to God?

ACTIVITY

Take three white socks that are similar in wear and dirt. The idea is to look at different means to clean the same thing.
1) Use no water and rub the dirt out.
2) Use water only and scrub.
3) Use soap/detergent and wash the sock.

Which one is cleaner? Picture yourself as the sock which process would you want God to use to clean your life.

This is how God works in us. It takes more time, cleansers, and effort but the results are where He wants us to be. Also, notice we cannot use fire to burn the impurities because it will harm the sock. God will not use a method that will hurt us. He only desires to make us clean for His will.

Personal Notes

Chapter 7
Service

Please read Matthew 5:1-16

"Ye are the light of the world. A city that is set on a hill cannot be hid." Matthew 5:14

God has created us to serve. We exist not by chance, but because He desired for us to be here. Everything has been ordained and planned by God. We are all given special gifts, talents, and the ability to use them for Him.

In Matthew chapter five, Jesus begins a sermon that starts with our character. Often people look at Matthew 5:3-12, which are called the Beatitudes, and try to point out the one closest to their character. This is not so. All Christians should exhibit all of the beatitudes which is no different than all Christians should have all of the fruits of the Spirit, (Galatians 5:22-23). God is revealing to us what it takes to become a complete person.

There will be moments when we show certain beatitudes at various times depending on the situation at hand. There are times where we have to be humble or comforted when we cry. We have to be meek and have a desire to build a stronger relationship with God. Sometimes we have to learn mercy and other moments the value of being pure.

Jesus especially wanted His disciples to hear this because they were actively working for Him. Granted, they were new and needed a lot of training, but they were active for God. No matter where we are, God can always use us. He will make sure to put us in the best possible situation to serve Him and experience success.

For example, if a person is new with the Bible, then God will not expect them to expound on all of the details of the Pauline epistles to a group of scholars in Cambridge. Instead, if a person only knows "In the beginning God created the heaven and the earth," Genesis 1:1, then He will put them in a place and time where they can share that knowledge with someone else. A friend might feel worthless because of the belief that humans are here by accident. However, by stating that God created everything, it puts hope in them that they are here for a purpose and this one encounter can change their life in a positive way.

With one text alone, a person can help millions of people, depending on how God uses them. The problem is not God, but us, who sometimes feel like our own problems will get in the way of the Master Creator's plans. The Lord has specifically made us so we can be of use to people.

Christ starts the sermon by giving examples of Christian character and than goes into a metaphor of service to the world. In this chapter we will focus more on how Jesus went into detail about us being the light of the world, (Matthew 5:14-16). This was the second metaphor used by Jesus as an example for people to spread the gospel.

Jesus wants us to shine for all people to see. He has placed a gift inside each person that was never meant to be hid, but to be shown for the entire world. Every single person born in this world has gifts that range from performance to being behind the scenes.

God Himself is the ultimate light source; we are to reflect that light to the world. Very much as the sun, which has its own method of taking fire and heat and making light, so does, God have His own glory and love to shine to the world. This love, like fire, is a powerful light for all those in darkness. What Jesus desires is the means to reflect this light to all people in the world.

In the solar system, our Moon reflects light from the Sun to the Earth. People who live in cities do not really get the full effect of a full moon lighting the streets because of the city lights that creates a glowing haze around the metropolitan area. However, in the country a full moon can light up the countryside. No, it is not as bright as the sun itself but it's enough that a person can see where they are going with careful steps. In addition, the moon is also a reminder that as long as it's glowing then the sun must be around and will return soon to light up the sky.

The same is with us. God has us as little moons for the world covered in darkness. On our own, we cannot shine the light, nor do we have the means. However when we get into the right spot, we can shine fully the love and message of Jesus to the world. Because it is reflecting off us, it is not perfect nor is it up to par as far as the heat and brightness of Jesus. All God asks is that we tell people of His soon return, (Matthew 28:18-20, Ezekiel 33:1-9). Much like the moon reveals that the sun is still operating and will be back around again, so we can reveal that Jesus is still working in the world and is soon to return.

We, being the light of the world, can be a reminder of God's love. Not necessarily on a global scale, but in our jobs, schools, families, neighborhoods, and even at church. We can affect the world by professing the name of Jesus not only with our mouths, but also in our lives and actions, (James 2:18-20). How we reflect Christ is how people will understand Him to be. Meaning, if we are overbearing and unapproachable then we show Christ as having similar qualities. Sometimes if we are judgmental, so people believe that Christ is the same way. Others think that Jesus is cliquish because we are like that. Then there are some instances when we force Jesus to people against their own will, and they believe that God is a demanding and forceful Being who takes away the power of choice.

All of these examples are errors in reflecting the character of God. We are not to force people, judge others, nor become overbearing. We must allow the Spirit to bring about conversion, not us. Remember that we do not have a Heaven to give them. It's not ours in the sense that we created it, but we can become tour guides and maps to our fellow brethren to Heaven as we travel along the way.

Our goal is to become like John the Baptist during the time of Christ living on Earth. "There was a man sent from God, whose name was John. The same came for a witness, to bear witness of the Light that, all men through him might believe. He was not the Light, but was sent to bear witness of that Light," John 1:6-8. Just like John, we are here to bear witness of the light of the world by showing our light that God has placed inside of us. We are not the light itself. God is the reason why we are here, not we ourselves. Living in a world full of evil and darkness, people are searching everywhere to see. The Lord is using Christians to guide others to Him so their paths, like ours, can be illuminated.

God desires us to shine our light, because the enemy is waiting to steal His lost sheep. "'For I am not pleased with the death of anyone who dies,' says the Lord God. 'So be sorry for your sins and turn away from them, and live,'" Ezekiel 18:32 (NLV). The Lord loves all people so no one is lost. It pains Him to see even one person not make it to Heaven.

"For His anger endureth but a moment; in His favor is life: weeping may endure for a night, but joy cometh in the morning," Psalms 30:5. God desires us to show the world joy. Right now while in darkness, it is hard to see when this will end. We as people do things that are wrong, because we are lost and feel like we are left to our own devices. Nevertheless, God is calling His people to put an end to this faulty line of thinking. He wants all people to have a chance at eternal life, (Ezekiel 33:11).

God's method of spreading His message of love is through us. Yes, we are imperfect beings with problems of our own, and we ourselves are trying to get to Heaven as well. However, God loves being able to use Divinity mixed in with humanity as a means of reaching all people. Jesus showed this in the ultimate sacrifice of becoming human while being fully Divine. His life was a constant example to all people through the ages in Heaven and Earth that when both sides come together amazing and marvelous things will happen.

The Lord has called people to allow themselves to be mixed with the Divine nature, not in the same way as Mary, mother of Jesus, but as light bearers like John the Baptist to spread the message of a gospel we should not be ashamed of, (Romans 1:16). Angels will not complete the work of spreading the message to the world. If God wanted the work accomplished by angels, He would have dispatched them already. Sometimes God sends Angels to help His people. The Lord has called us as people to do the work, and believing that another person or being will do it is laziness and goes against God's principle.

The Lord has a variety of ways of being able to spread His gospel to the world. The most common way we think of is through preaching and singing. However, to some are given the gift of prophesy and discernment. Others are able to organize and have the gift of hospitality. Some people can love unconditionally or others have a natural ability to draw in children and youth. Several people will be given the power to heal, while others will have a stronger temperance so they can be examples to others.

A few are called to be local leaders or disciples in our cities. Others will have to take their message to other states and some to lands across the world. We are not here to judge one another, but realize that every person is called to do something for God. The amount of people that is lead to Baptism is not important, as long as we are doing what Christ has called us to do.

God is ecstatic when we choose to have our light shine for all people. We are the candlestick and He will light us with his Spiritual fire. As we go about spreading God's message, our light will light other candlesticks that are connected to Christ while we never lose our own power. Then these people will go and do the same, and it is all because we were more than willing to let our light shine and be of use.

Jesus said when responding to His disciples on the events of the end of the world, "The Good News about the holy nation of God must be preached over all the earth. It must be told to all nations and then the end will come," Matthew 24:14 (NLV). Yes throughout the 24th chapter of Matthew there are warnings of plagues, problems, iniquity, wars, and various other bad situations that will arise. However, these are all signs of the end. The truth is that Jesus will return when the Gospel will be preached over the entire world.

Jesus wants us to go out into our communities, cities, and even the world because all people should have an opportunity to know God. By spreading the good news of Jesus return, we would have done our part, and will have to wait for God's soon return.

We must remember not to treat it like the crusades. Forcing people to love the Lord is not His plan. We error when we try to force people to love the Lord. God is all-powerful and if he wanted to force obedience, He would have done so already. Instead, He decided to die for our sins so that we can choose Him. Life ever lasting is available to all; however, many will not choose that path. All we can do is leave them in God's hands and hope they will reconsider God before it is too late. He only requires that we do our job for Him.

It is almost like a check mark system in that God desires for the entire world to be saved. Not all people will choose Him. Our job is to make sure that each person on Earth has the right amount of information and knowledge about the true nature and character of Christ. People must be able to witness and explore the love of Jesus for themselves so they can accurately make the decision to follow or not. The hard job of converting will only come by the means and power of the Holy Spirit.

God will provide the means for all people to do His will. We have a system called the internet, which allows us to provide information and knowledge to all people from around the world. We have the Olympic Games, the World Cup in various sports, and many other attractions that brings the world together in one place for peace. The United Nations is a worldwide organization set on uplifting peace and prosperity of life to all nations. The list goes on about what we have at our disposal to be able to get the Gospel of Christ to the world.

The disciples on boats, horseback and just their sandals reached most of the known world because of their strong desire to reach all people about the soon return of Jesus. God led them to go to certain key people so they would spread it in their own nation.

For example, Philip was used by God to spread the message of Christ to the Ethiopians, (Acts 8:26-40). Paul was sent to various countries and cities around the world to spread the gospel to leaders and citizens. In spite of various groups trying to stop them, the light of Jesus Christ still shined through the entire world and even now, in various cultures and countries where

Christianity is not practiced; there are still certain moral beliefs that are inherited in their society.

God has called us to be a light bearer for Him. There is a fire on the inside that will shine through, but only if we allow God to use the talents and skills He has blessed us with. Sometimes we do not believe we have talents, but we all do. God has not created anybody without some type of skill.

We need to look at what comes naturally. Is it gift-giving or entertaining people at your home? Some have a higher affinity for people, or can teach complicated ideas clearly. Inside of others is the desire to take care of children effortlessly, or we might have the gift of music and art. We should ask co-workers, friends, schoolmates, church members, and even family what they see in us. This might help us see what talents and abilities we may have.

As you begin to mature in Christ, the Lord will start to use you with these gifts and others that He will give you as you proceed in life. Soon, just as you thought you had none, now you have two, five, ten, or more and all are being used for Jesus.

The light that you shine is not your own, but the power of God dwelling inside of you. Let it glow. Do not hide or cover it up, but let others see it, because just like you do not have the desire to live in darkness, neither do they.

Build a firm foundation by knowing and acting on the fact, that God has not created you by accident, but you are here with a purpose. Your purpose is to serve the Lord, and by doing so, your life will be enhanced more then you can imagine.

Quoted Scripture

Matthew 5:14 Ye are the light of the world. A city that is set on a hill cannot be hid
Genesis 1:1 In the beginning God created the heaven and the earth
John 1:6-8 The same came for a witness, to bear witness of the Light
Ezekiel 18:32 For I am not pleased with the death of anyone who dies (NLV)
Psalms 30:5 Weeping may endure for a night, but joy cometh in the morning
Matthew 24:14 The Good News about the holy nation of God must be preached

Scripture for Future Study

Ezekiel 33:1-9 A watchmen for God
Ezekiel 33:11 God desires for all people to live
Matthew 5:3-12 Beatitudes
Matthew 5:14-16 We are the Light of the world
Matthew 24 Signs of Christ return
Matthew 28:18-20 Tell people of Jesus soon return
Romans 1:16 Not ashamed of the Gospel
Galatians 5:22-23 Fruits of the Spirit
James 2:14-26 Faith with works

STUDY GUIDE

1.)   Name a reason why we are created?
FOTF Pg 105

Write out the beatitudes from Matthew 5:3-12. When or how can you exhibit each one?

verse 3 _____

_____

verse 4 _____

_____

verse 5 _____

_____

verse 6 _____

_____

verse 7 _____

_____

verse 8 _____

_____

verse 9 _____

_____

verse 10 _____

_____

verse 11_____

_____

2.)   On page 106 there is an example by using Genesis 1:1 and how it can be used to teach
        someone. Give one text you know or like and how you can use that to teach someone.

3.)   What example is given as those who are to shine the light on the world?
FOTF Pg 106

4.)   What character trait do you have that reflects God to people?

5.)   What characteristics can we have that will negatively influence those we are trying
        to represent God to?
FOTF Pg 107

6.)   What was John the Baptist mission? How is this similar to the current job for the
       Church to the World?
John 1:6-8, FOTF Pg 107

7.)   What is something that God is not pleased? What is His desire?
Ezekiel 18:32, FOTF Pg 107

8.)   What is God's plan for spreading His message? What is the example He gave to us?
FOTF Pg 108

9.)   Will angels complete the job?
FOTF Pg 108

10.)   When talking about the end of the world, what did Jesus say to His disciples? What
         is the true symbol or time when the end will come?
Matthew 24:14, FOTF Pg 109

11.)   What method should we not use and why?
FOTF Pg 109

12.)   What will God provide for people to be successful? What advancements has been
         given to this generation to tell about the love of Christ and His soon return to the
         world?
FOTF Pg 109-110

PERSONAL STUDY

1.)   What talents do you have and what things do you enjoy doing?

2.)   What possible service/job do you believe God is calling you to do? What steps can you take to about fulfilling that calling?

ACTIVITY

Ask five different people of various backgrounds the top three talents and characteristics they see in you. Compare what they all say and see if there's any common ground. Also, take note of who said what. Maybe they see something in you because you behave or think differently.

Then be honest with yourself, what things do you genuinely enjoy. Do you like some of the things they said or did they pick out something that you didn't realize?

Now that you're building an idea of your skill set as well as character traits, ask God for an opportunity to use them. It might be fast or it might take some time, but go out there and start being productive for the Lord.

Remember to learn and allow growth to occur. You might be called to be a preacher, but first you have to be a member of a small ministry in church just to get some basic practice and knowledge.

A.) _____

_____

B.) _____

_____

C.) _____

_____

D.) _____

_____

E.) _____

_____

Personal Notes

Chapter 8
Baptism with the Holy Spirit part 1

Please read Matthew 3:7-12

"...He shall baptize you with the Holy Ghost, and with fire." Matthew 3:11

Imagine taking the gifts and talents you already posses and magnifying them by a thousand. This is the result of what will happen when the Holy Spirit begins to have His way in our lives. John the Baptist knew the results of giving people baptism by immersion in water.

Baptism is a symbol of being born again. "I say unto thee, Except a man be born again, he cannot see the kingdom of God," John 3:3. Jesus, when talking to Nicodemus, refers to the symbolic transformation of giving one's life to Christ. A person must show that they are willing to change and become a new creature for the Lord. We are born into sin and evil is all around us, meaning we are evil as well.

However, God made a way out of that situation by allowing us to be born again. Obviously, the Lord never meant that a person had to reenter the womb as Nicodemus mustered up, but we must simply be immersed in water and come up again. This immersion process is the symbol of a person dying into a grave and coming out alive by the Spirit. To the Lord, a person must transform their character to enter the gates of Heaven.

The watery immersion also refers to the cleansing of our character. Water is of course used as a cleaning agent for just about everything. By going down into the water, we accept the cleaning power of the Lord and come out renewed and fresh, ready to serve Him.

How important is baptism? Jesus participated in the act of baptism by immersion, Matthew 3:13-17. John was at first nervous to baptize Jesus knowing who He was, but Jesus wanted to set an example that all people need to be baptized. Even though He was perfect, Jesus was still baptized.

We may look at baptism as being used for a means of cleansing oneself from sin, which is true and should be used for that. There are other times when you can use baptism as a means of getting closer to God by being born of the Spirit through going down into the watery grave. Many married couples go down together as a symbol of giving up their past as individuals and starting a new life as a couple.

When Jesus was baptized, it was one of the rare occasions mentioned in the Bible where God the Father, God the Son, and God the Holy Spirit all share the space at the same time on Earth. This is how important Baptism is for people it brings unity amongst the Trinity. Jesus' baptism brought on the Spirit in the form of a dove while God the Father proclaimed, "This is my beloved Son, in whom I am well pleased," Matthew 3:17.

Quoted Scripture

Matthew 3:11 He shall baptize you with the Holy Ghost, and with fire
John 3:3 Except a man be born again, he cannot see the kingdom of God
Matthew 3:17 This is my beloved Son, in whom I am well pleased

Scripture for Future Study

Matthew 3:13-17 Jesus is baptized

STUDY GUIDE

1.)   What does Baptism symbolizes?
John 3:3, FOTF Pg 119

2.)   We cannot physically be born again, so what was Christ talking about?
FOTF Pg 119

3.)   What does immersion symbolizes?
FOTF Pg 120

4.)   If Jesus was perfect and He was baptized, that means that Baptism does not only have to be for cleansing of sin. What else can it be used for? Remember that this is a symbol of being renewed in Christ.
FOTF Pg 120

PERSONAL STUDY

1.)   Why did Jesus choose to be baptized?

2.)   Jesus talks about being born again to Nicodemus. How important is the rebirth of our character to make it to Heaven? When reflecting on childbirth, how can your personal character change be reborn as it relates to this process?

ACTIVITY

We will look at baptism and the birth of a new spiritual character by examining two different videos. First, go to the internet, video store, a video links place like YouTube, or anywhere else where you can see people being baptize and child birthing.

First, see the child birthing. For as long as you can watch it, note the process and all that is involved. It takes a lot of care to deliver a baby, and it takes even more effort to help raise the child. Look at the baby as the birth of a person's new character. Would changing your character be easy? Is there work involved to keep it inline to where it is suppose to be? Describe other similarities.

Then see some baptisms. Take note on what it looks like, the joy, what is happening, and how the audience or people are responding. Praise God, we do not have to be born again like the birthing video you just saw, but being baptize can bring upon the same character change. Just remember that it takes work to keep you where God desires. You do not get baptize and then without any work live perfectly. You have to stay in the Lord, daily.

Write your notes on…

1.) Birthing

2.) Baptism

Personal Notes

Chapter 9
Baptism with the Holy Spirit part 2

Please read Acts 1:3-8

"God is light, and in Him is no darkness at all." 1 John 1:5

John the Baptist used baptism to bring people into the faith but always knew that a greater and stronger power would come after him. John knew that Jesus would come to this Earth with the power to baptize people with the Holy Spirit.

"But ye shall receive power, after that the Holy Ghost is come upon you: and ye shall be witnesses unto me both in Jerusalem, and in all Judaea, and in Samaria, and unto the uttermost part of the earth," Acts 1:8. Jesus gave this promise to the disciples. The Holy Spirit could only come after Jesus had left the world. Jesus knew that the mission He had for them could only be accomplished with the power of the Holy Spirit working and dwelling within them.

Until this time, the disciples had accomplished many things. They where able to heal people, cast demons, preach the gospel of Christ, and take part in various teaching from the Master Rabbi Himself. In the human form, Christ could only be with the disciples at one place at a time. However, Christ gave them a special power from Heaven in the form of a Spirit. The disciples would now be able to have the presence of Christ no matter where they go, and all of them would have equal access.

God desires to be with us in the same manner. He wants to be with us, our families, friends, strangers, all at once, and yet individually as though you are the only person on this planet. The Holy Spirit is here so all will have that same personal experience the disciples had while Christ was on Earth. For them, Jesus was their power source for healings and teachings. Now that Christ went back to Heaven, the Lord sent another in the form of a Spirit so that all would have equal access to the source, and the ministry can get to the entire world at one time.

The use of the word Ghost and Spirit really refers to His omnipresence. He can be everywhere and be with each individual person as though He is only with him or her in a one on one situation. The Holy Spirit is not scary or ghastly like zombies and specters, which are creatures from the grave. This Being of Spirituality is all about representing Christ to the fullest and allowing us inside knowledge about God.

"Howbeit when He, the Spirit of truth, is come, He will guide you into all truth: for He shall not speak of Himself; but whatsoever He shall hear, that shall He speak: and He will shew you things to come. He shall glorify Me: for he shall receive of Mine, and shall shew it unto you," John 16:13-14. Christ is making it clear that the Holy Spirit is all about continuing the same message, gospel, and power of Jesus so this world will have an opportunity to choose Him. There is truth and knowledge that the Spirit plans on sharing and it is for us freely if we decide to plug into what He is showing us.

To be baptized in the Holy Spirit means there is an immersion into whom He is. It is almost like water; His presence wraps and covers us. This means that we change into Spirit filled beings instead of flesh and that our faults burn away instead of just being cleansed. Being washed by water is good, but to be molded by fire is even better.

The Holy Spirit even provides a boost of energy to all those who listen to His teachings. Like fire gives power to those things that are adapted to take it, so will the Spirit give you that extra energy. He works like a catalyst to the believer because the knowledge of Christ is already implanted. Christ has made sure that the world gets some type of knowledge about Him, especially through people like ourselves who go out and represent Him to whomever we meet. The Holy Spirit than takes that knowledge of Christ and begins to work on it, feeding the fuel of truth and understanding while empowering the person with love.

As a new believer begins to learn more about Christ, there is a rush, much like the Ephesus church, (Revelations 2:1-7), where a believer wants to do all they can to spread the gospel. Notice how new believers are the most excited in church or willing to do anything. See how the new people respond to every word that drips from the pulpit as if it's a holiday dinner.

They love it and want more, because the Holy Spirit is actively pushing all the right buttons to get an immediate response to the message of God.

This is why sometimes even those who have an experience in the church for decades can all of a sudden burst out into excitement when the Holy Ghost touches them. Sometimes it is through instant praising, clapping, dancing, crying, and other forms of celebrations because the Spirit reveals numerous times when Christ has brought us through or is currently working in our lives.

As fire can be combustible, so can the interaction of the Spirit with those who choose to use Him. In Acts 2:1-13 tells of a time where the disciples begin to preach to people of various language backgrounds and when they spoke, every man understood them in their own tongue. At first, they were confused, but the people were captivated by the words that Peter preached and 3000 people joined the church that day.

This is the power and fire of the Spirit working inside of someone who chooses to let Him. Where we might gain a soul to be baptized, with the Holy Spirit, 20 might join. Three people might clap their hands when we sing, whereas with the spirit an entire church will praise the Lord for minutes because of His touching. There are plenty other cases and examples that we can use, but remember that our next level of power can only come from the Spirit. To ignore Him is to commit the unpardonable sin, (Matthew 12:31-32). We cannot deny access of the Holy Ghost to our heart, because He is the mediator between Christ and us. He connects us to Christ because He fully represents our Savior. By saying we have no desire of the Spirit is saying we have no desire of Jesus Christ.

We can build a strong foundation in Christ by turning to the Spirit and allowing Him to speak truth into our lives. It is our only way to be effective in this world of darkness. Christ guarantees our success by sending the Holy Spirit into our lives. He has no desire for us to fail. Jesus sends the Spirit not only to speak truth and give us energy but to comfort us as well. We can feel secure in knowing that God is stronger than all possible dangers. Jesus knows that there will be times of struggle and He wants to reassure His sheep that He is there with us like our home, vehicle, friends, family, and the lamp in our room or the trees outside. Christ is right there like air that passes through our lungs. We may not be able to see it but its effects are real and unquestioned.

When we desire to have the spirit within us, we automatically exhibit certain attributes that spring forth. "The fruit of the Spirit is love, joy, peace, longsuffering, gentleness, goodness, faith, meekness, temperance, against such there is no law," Galatians 5:22-23. We cannot select the fruits of the Spirit but realize that we are to exhibit all of them to be a complete Christian. With the Holy Ghost fire dwelling in us, all nine of these fruits will grow and blossom out of us at the right time. Remember that the Holy Spirit is cultivating in us these fruits so that we can serve.

At different stages in our lives, we will exhibit each fruit depending on the situation. There might be a time when we will need peace in the midst of arguments. Love might be instituted for those who are family, friends, or strangers. Often we have to have faith in the midst of adversity or temperance so we do not gorge ourselves on things that are a blessing.

The Lord is complete and His desire to make us whole is evident because He sent His Spirit to help us grow. He wants every person, albeit in His fold or not, to be able to have a chance to be with Him in glory. This is why it was so important for Christ to send the Holy Spirit, because He loves all people and wanted to make sure that everyone has a chance to get to know Him personally like the disciples. He loves you, the Spirit is available to expound on the character and love of Christ, just let Him in, and He will show you. Allow the Spirit to dwell in you and build a strong relationship in Jesus Christ.

Quoted Scripture

1 John 1:5 God is light, and in Him is no darkness at all
Acts 1:8 Ye shall receive power, after that the Holy Ghost is come upon you
John 16:13-14 The Spirit of truth, is come, He will guide you into all truth
Galatians 5:22-23 The fruit of the Spirit

Scripture for Future Study

Matthew 12:31-32 The unpardonable sin
Acts 2:1-13 Holy Spirit is upon the Disciples, they speak in many languages
Revelations 2:1-7 God's message to the Ephesians

STUDY GUIDE

1.)   What power was promised to the disciples? Why did it have to wait for Jesus to physically leave the earth?

FOTF Pg 126

2.)   What were the limitations of Christ as a person on earth? In Spirit what is the major difference?

FOTF Pg 126

3.)   Ghost and Spirit are often used when referring the omnipresence of God. What does this mean and how should we be encouraged in knowing this ability of God?

FOTF Pg 127

4.)   What will the Spirit of Truth come to do?
John 16:13-14, FOTF Pg 127

5.)   What does it mean to be immersed in the Spirit? How is this similar and different then watery immersion?
FOTF Pg 127

6.)   What are some of the action that can happen when touched by the Spirit?
FOTF Pg 128

7.)   What is the unpardonable sin? What is the connection between Jesus?
Matthew 12:31-32, FOTF Pg 128

PERSONAL STUDY

1.)   How is the Holy Spirit a gift to all people?

ACTIVITY

Below is a list of the Fruits of the Spirit as found in Galatians 5:22-23. Explain what each characteristic means and how can you exhibit each trait.

Love

Joy

Peace

Longsuffering

Gentleness

Goodness

Faith

Meekness

Temperance

Personal Notes

Chapter 10
Trial by Fire pt 1

Please read Daniel 3:1-7

"When you walk through fire, you will not be burned, nor will the flames hurt you." Isaiah 43:2 (NCV)

There is a difference between the flames that God has prepared and fire from humanity. We have read where God desires to burn off the harmful traits of our characters so we can be better disciples and Christians for Him, (Foundation of the Fire chapters 5 and 6). If we have a drinking problem, He wants to cure it, if we have low self-esteem God will raise it, whatever our problem is God wants to fix it. The simile of fire is used because it is complete. Once you burn gold, silver or iron then it remains that way until fire changes its form. Also, by using fire, we can burn out the impurities so the metal is pure and valuable.

Humanity's fire causes harm and hurt. There is scarring and problems that come with human's fire. We use fire for death with guns, cannons, and missiles. At the time of Shadrach, Meshach, and Abednego, it meant a furnace.

King Nebuchadnezzar decided to build himself an image, (Daniel 3:1-7), for worship. He set it on a hill and got leadership behind it so that the people of the land would worship this giant golden statue. He even made a decree that when the music starts all people must worship the image and whoever does not, will die.

In our time, we may not have anyone in particular erecting large images of themselves and force people to worship it, but we do have similar situations that are present. Instead of a large golden statue, sometimes leadership will start a false belief and have everyone follow that.

The image the world uses is anything that a group of people or a single person institutes in our lives that goes against what God has told us to believe. The image that the leadership would want us to follow will of course come with certain aspects to make worshipping that image more attractive. Just as King Nebuchadnezzar did, there are practices that the world will establish to force people in following their rules instead of God's standard.

1) King Nebuchadnezzar made the image large and attractive. It was approximately 90 feet tall, and covered in gold. Imagine a statue that would stand as tall as a basketball court is long that is overlaid with gold. Then set it on a hill so it could gleam and sparkle in the sunlight to draw everyone's eyes to behold and worship.

The world is no different in presenting ideas and "images" that are very attractive. For example, the idea to get money at all cost, instead of a sense of community and family. The idea that self overrides all, including God. We are shown how certain people are living large and how we should have a desire to have the same object. The world will make these ideas sound like they are the best thing for us and that if we follow then it will help us. The idea that if we where rich then all of our dreams will come true.

Not to say that getting money is wrong, because it's not. The desire for money is wrong when it becomes the only course for living and it consumes all thoughts. There is nothing wrong with having confidence, but getting cocky and arrogant will lead us away from what God wants, (Ezekiel 16:15). Showing people a better way to live is one thing, forcing them to do it is another. We have to realize that just because the world will show flashy images of people and say we can be happy like them, does not mean that even those people are happy, nor does it mean that their lifestyle will bring us any joy. Always see what the world is saying compare to what God is saying. A ring that glitters on one person's hand might be dull on another.

Food allergies are an example of how an item can be good for one person but harmful to another. Some people love peanuts and will eat them in cookies, oils, and spreads. However, others are allergic to peanuts and a little oil from this legume can cause sickness and death.

We marvel at other people's success and mirror exactly what they do and who they are. Their success could be tailored for them and not work for all people. Because someone made their money being in front of an audience or on stage, doesn't mean another with stage fright can follow the same path, (Proverbs 4:14-19). God knows exactly what we need to be successful. Use Him and not the false images of others.

2) Leadership will get behind the plan of a new idea or image. Humans are intrinsically programmed to follow leaders. Sometimes it can be anywhere from climbing Mount Everest to war or even to death in a belief that comets or Kool Aid will save them. If we believe the leader is strong and smart and they follow the image or promote it, then sometimes we will follow suit. King Nebuchadnezzar made sure that his governors, princes, judges, and sheriffs were on one accord with worshipping the golden image. He knew that people would follow and would want to be a part of the worship experience because their own personal leader was showing the example that it was okay.

Do not be fooled just because leadership is going head over hills for some plan we know God says is wrong. Just because someone is powerful does not mean they will use it to benefit others. "Beware of false prophets, which come to you in sheep's clothing, but inwardly they are ravening wolves," Matthew 7:15. Some leaders are in this world to do harm and will lead you to destruction. We must know for ourselves that God wants us to follow a leader who is following Jesus. If confused, then go to the Bible and consult God. Remember that people do not have a Heaven for us to go to, God does.

3) Another ploy that the King used was playing music to stir up emotions and it was the symbol to worship the golden statue. Once the music was heard the people knew it was time to let themselves go and worship their new god.

The world, government, organizations, or people in general are all about playing on people's emotions. They know that if we get emotional then we will go out and do things that had we stopped to think about it, we would never have done. One of the greatest examples of this is the Holocaust. There was huge Nazi propaganda on how Jews were the enemy and they were the reason for Germany's defeat in the World War 1. Many people blamed the Jews for the country's economic downturn and various other problems in Germany. Because of that, people killed, raped, experimented, starved, or did other atrocities until six million people had died. Why? Because the overwhelming propaganda was built on hate, due to racial differences.

This is why God gave us the sense of reason and tells us to be patient. If we react to propagandas, as in the case of Germany, people get hurt. God gave us that ability to think things through before doing something as extreme as killing millions. For most of us, the taking of lives is not in our vocabulary but we are prone to do something out of character.

We could find ourselves in bed with someone we shouldn't be in bed with, doing drugs, stealing money from the company because others are, speaking untruths in church because others believe them, and there are many other examples.

Stop for a moment and think. There are times when we have to respond quickly, but those are in cases of danger. Outside of that, we must allow God to control our emotional center. Jesus should direct us in all matters so that when the time comes, we do not have to fall down and worship the false image because we hear the music, or see the propaganda.

4) The King knew that some would not worship just because of the attractiveness of the image, the leadership response, or because of the music. He puts in the last part of the decree that states anyone who does not worship will be thrown into the fiery furnace. He made worship of the image a law for that country.

There might be times where the law of the land might not fit well with God's plan. There are times where a community or church might force an ideal because they believe it's the right thing to do. For example the idea that we have to be excited and support a war that is going on or in some places, we are forced not to support the war. There are people who support hating others because of race, ethnic background, beliefs, sexual preference, or social standing. At other times, we promote getting money and financial success over having a healthy family life.

The image that is set up can be different for various people depending on where we live and what organization it's coming from. In the time of Babylon, this came straight from the King. Currently it can come from the government, church, school, our job, or even community and social organizations.

Notice how various groups with structure have the ability to create an image. Governments can do it in the form of propaganda and even as extreme as making laws. For example, the Holocaust, drafting troops when citizens are against the war, slavery, and making laws that force people to believe a certain way. Social groups and organizations can make unwanted changes. We hear about hazing in Greek fraternities and sororities. There could be an organization, which is set up to help all people but instead they only choose to help certain ethnicities.

Churches can also follow this method by forcing people to believe in bringing more people to the edifice instead of having a genuine relationship with God. There are times when churches begin to preach what is not in the Bible, which of course means we have to study for ourselves and compare what God says to the church teachings, (Isaiah 28:9-14, 2 Timothy 2:15). Do not follow all churches just because its leaders sound good. Most churches are here to help the community and foster a relationship with God. Remember that our foundation should be in what the Bible states and not what people say.

God's standard is The Standard. Measure everything against that. Of course, in church it is easier because we are using the Bible to hold it up against an organization who also believes in the truth of God's word. Depend on God to see what He would have us to do in all cases such as school, work, or family issues.

It is tough because like the Babylonians; we would want a sense of connection to the group. There is a pull to conform even though it goes against what you know is right because most people do not desire to be an outcast. Become that outcast yourself. People should not pull you in the direction that you do not want to go. If you know that God has something for you, and desires you to follow it, then by stepping on His side you can be more of a leader and bring about change than if you just go along with the mob mentality.

What God has for you, is what you need to live by and not what people have to say. By doing this you can make yourself stick out, not for self but because you are representing God. By showing a little light to people, all of a sudden changes in mindset and character to those around you can take place. Not all people will want to conform, don't worry about them. Be who Jesus wants you to be and let Him worry about others.

Quoted Scripture

Isaiah 43:2 When you walk through fire, you will not be burned (NCV)
Matthew 7:15 Beware of false prophets, which come to you in sheep's clothing

Scripture for Future Study

Proverbs 4:14-19 Do not follow in the ways of the wicked
Isaiah 28:9-14 Study the entire Bible
Ezekiel 16:15 Becoming arrogant in yourself
Daniel 3:1-7 Nebuchadnezzar builds an image of gold
2 Timothy 2:15 Study to show yourself approved

STUDY GUIDE

1.)   What is the difference between God's fire and humanity's?
FOTF Pg 137

2.)   What did the King decide at the beginning of Daniel 3?
Daniel 3:1

3.)   List the practices that King Nebuchadnezzar did to make people follow his plan over God's? Then write an example of how that same practice could be used today?

A.) **FOTF Pg 138**

B.) **FOTF Pg 139**

C.) **FOTF Pg 139-140**

D.) **FOTF Pg 140**

4.)   Next to each organization below write how they can create an image, idol, law, rule, or tradition that is not according to God's plan.

Government

Church

Social Group

(You Choose)

5.)   What is the standard that we should live our lives and why?
FOTF Pg 141

6.)   If God has a plan for you, should you go with that or go according to society?

PERSONAL STUDY

1.)   What images in society are we being influenced to worship? What ways can we take a stand?

2.)   How can relying on self lead us to go against God's standard for all people? What ways can we learn God's standard and apply them in our lives?

ACTIVITY

Below are examples of different people in various situations. Each person is confronted with a choice. Read the statement and write out what you think they should do, and what God's will would be for them? Also write what you would do if confronted in the same situation.

1.)   Tyrone joined a local social organization because of their promise to help the community. There were no stipulations so he figured that all people would be helped. However, once there, he realizes that they are only targeting a select group and ignoring others because of an assumption they are not worthy for our help. Tyrone wants to leave but does enjoy helping others. He wants to convince them that since they're gaining money for a grant to help all people that is what they should do. Tyrone is unsure if he should leave, tell the grant providers, or start his own organization.

2.)   Mary loves to look her best but sometimes she allows it to change her personality. Especially when it comes to the choice of finger nail polish. She is very meticulous and believes her hands are the best she's ever seen. Mary believes that just a few days ago, God told her not to wear finger nail polish because of the pompous attitude it kept bringing up in her. Her new pride was swelling up every time she puts some on, and God informed her that it was a thorn into her ministry so she can represent Him to those she's supposed to be ministering. Mary doesn't feel like anyone else has to stop, just her because of her own personal feelings. However, this announcement came after she bought a new set of finger nail polish. She's unsure if she should throw them away or try to change her attitude when she puts on the decorative paint. (In your case, God might be telling you something that personal he wants you to give up, because it's blocking you from him.)

3.) Victor is a recovering alcoholic who lost his money, family, and self-respect due to a ten-year addiction. His wife left him, because he would become abusive. His job fired him due to poor performance and he hates himself because of being arrested for public intoxication. Victor is thrilled that he's never got behind the wheel and compounded his problems. Now that Victor has gotten over his addiction he is a new man and feels great about himself. He hasn't had a drink in six months although the cravings show up periodically. Victor has joined a church but is hesitant to join in communion. Not because of his relationship with God, but due to the fact that this church serves real wine during communion. He doesn't know if he should sip the wine and continue to miss communion, or find a church that does not use real wine.

4.)   A new law has been passed in Amy's state that they're no longer allowed to publically serve God. This is because it was an offense to someone, so the state requires that there will no longer be public worship. If anyone is found worshiping in public or in a church, they will be tried and sent to prison. Amy loves to worship God and have always looked forward to worshiping amongst people. Should Amy stay and worship with others who will defy the law, or should she move in fear of being sent to prison?

Personal Notes

Chapter 11
Trial By Fire part 2

Please read Daniel 3:8-12

"The Lord is my light and my salvation; whom shall I fear?" Psalms 27:1

In Daniel 3:8-12, certain men under the King's command went to Nebuchadnezzar and reported to him that not all people were worshipping the image the King made. These men pointed out Shadrach, Meshach, and Abednego, which was truly hurtful to the King because of his relationship with them.

It has to be understood that there were a variety of conquered people from all races, countries, and beliefs in Babylon. Probably not everyone fell in love with this new image but played along. There were those who truly believed the new image to be the standard and god, where as some probably bowed but prayed to their own god or just simply were lost in thought. The three Hebrew men mentioned in the Bible decided against the appearance of worshipping a false image. For them to bow was against what they knew to be true, which was the Great Jehovah in Heaven.

This is an example of standing up for God. The three Hebrew men could have bowed to the image but prayed to God in Heaven, but they chose not to. The trio cared less of what the King thought and wanted to make sure that God would not be offended.

The mindset they had is what we should have. Going along with the flow so we do not make anyone mad is ludicrous. God expects us to stand for Him and not give in to any false images. Of course, it's hard to stand for the Lord. Yes, there are people, like the King's men, who will be there to point us out.

In our case, it could be a co-worker, fellow student, a sibling, church member, neighbor, or even a friend. Many people will bring us down in a moment, because they believe it will help them out in the future. They will do all they can to please people around them so they themselves can have a promotion or be looked upon with favor by the group.

Ignore these people and their words. We should do what is necessary for God not for self. It does not matter if we are on the church board or at work. We can be in a study group for a class final or in a Greek Fraternity meeting. It does not matter. Everywhere we go, we have certain principles and a moral makeup that God has instituted in us. "I will put my teachings in their minds and write them on their hearts. I will be their God, and they will be my people," Jeremiah 31:33 (NCV). The feeling and sense of knowing what's right and wrong will come naturally if we would allow God to manifest Himself in us.

Our foundation is in the Rock. This means we cannot and will not be moved. God will anchor us so the storms of life will never break us down. God is there to make sure that we come out of every situation on top. Allow Him to deal with those who try to do you harm.

King Nebuchadnezzar was hurt especially since these three men came under his tutelage back in Daniel chapter 1. It was here where after the King had chosen specific people from the Hebrews that were given the opportunity to learn the Chaldeans language, arts, and science that Shadrach, Meshach, Abednego, and Daniel were all chosen to be trained as leaders in the government and were given food and wine for strength.

These four guys did not want to eat the King's food because it went against what God had set aside for them. Of course, there was much trouble with this because had they become weaker, Melzar, the man appointed over them, would have been killed, (Daniel 1:10). They reassured Melzar that everything would be okay, and after they had the food prescribed for them by God, they where healthier and better off than everyone else, (Daniel 1:12-13).

This test was the beginning for these men to stand up to the local authority in the name of God and do what was right. The food change got back to King Nebuchadnezzar and they were appointed as various leaders in his court.

God will give each person the opportunity to stand for Him in little things before moving to a harder challenge. For the three Hebrew men, it was the power to choose their food. For us it could be not to smoke before we tackle matters at our job or the ability to stand up at church meetings before we take on the government. Whatever it is, God will never send anyone in a situation without giving them some type of experience. The Lord guarantees our success, (Joshua 6:2).

The Lord believes in building our confidence in Him, so we will know He is there for us. God desires to make Himself real in our life just as we can touch our clothes. He is right there and has our best possible interest for our lives in mind.

The Lord blessed Shadrach, Meshach, and Abednego for standing up and doing things His way. They were allowed to learn knowledge in there respective fields so they could represent God the best possible way. God was teaching them spiritual matters, but the Chaldeans taught them in other forms. The three Hebrew men and Daniel were able to gain the greatest amount of knowledge at that time and then filtered it through God's teaching.

During our lifetime, God will provide the means for us, His people, to gain the best possible knowledge for our career. If we are a doctor, then God will allow us to go to the best schools and gain information from the best possible medical institution. If we are an administrative assistant, then God will bless us with the wisdom to become the best assistant for our boss. For historians the ability to find the right books will be because the Holy Spirit is leading us; or if we are a bus driver then God will allow our eyesight to be keener so we can transport people safely to their destinations.

By standing up for God, you will be elevated at your career. The Lord will push you forward because He only wants the best for you. If He wants you to be a manager or supervisor, then you will be there. If God chooses you to start your own company or yearns for you to be CEO of some established Fortune 500 company then God will place you there as well. The more you lift up God the more He will lift you up.

This not only goes for your career but in other aspects of your life, for example, in church you can gain a higher position on the board. If you are in a social organization, they might promote you because they see you as a strong leader and lead the group to a better place. In your family, you can gain more respect and be called on for times of need. God is there to bless you and to raise you up, and it all starts by following Him.

Quoted Scripture

Psalms 27:1 The Lord is my light and my salvation; whom shall I fear
Jeremiah 31:33 I will put my teachings in their minds (NCV)

Scripture for Future Study

Joshua 6:2 God promised victory for the Israelites
Daniel 1 The first test for Daniel and the three Hebrew men
Daniel 3:8-12 King's men report that the three Hebrew men did not bow

STUDY GUIDE

1.)   Read **Daniel 2:46-49**. Who was appointed and what was there position?

2.)   Would the Chaldean leadership been mad to see conquered people at those positions?

3.)   Now re-read **Daniel 3:8-12**. Why would these men go after Shadrach, Meshach, and Abednego but leave Daniel alone? (Look at verse 49 in Daniel 2)

4.)   What do you call people who try to bring you down? Do you think jealousy brought on revenge?

5.)   How could the three Hebrew men hide and make sure they where in no danger? Why didn't they do this?
FOTF Pg 152

6.)   What is instituted within us?
Jeremiah 31:33, FOTF Pg 153

7.)   Why shouldn't we be worry about those who come against us?
FOTF Pg 153

8.)   What test was given to the men in standing up for God?
Daniel 1, FOTF Pg 153

9.)   What will God give us before we can grow spiritually?
FOTF Pg 154

10.)   What will God provide for His people?
FOTF Pg 154

PERSONAL STUDY

1.)   The Lord builds us up over time to handle the stresses we are going through currently. What trial/struggle have you gone through and overcame that can help you with whatever situation you are in currently?

2.)   There are always people who are trying to take you down. How can this be a symbol of you doing what is right and what ways can you handle these people?

ACTIVITY

Create a web of influence.

This will show you how you can help many people and see what your web of influence is. We want to look at this not only from where you are now but where you're going to be.

Remember that God elevates His people so He can get the glory and to help others. Below is a rough example of a web, but look at chapter seven and the traits you've written down as well as people you interact with from chapter four. The next few pages have been provided so you can do multiple ones.

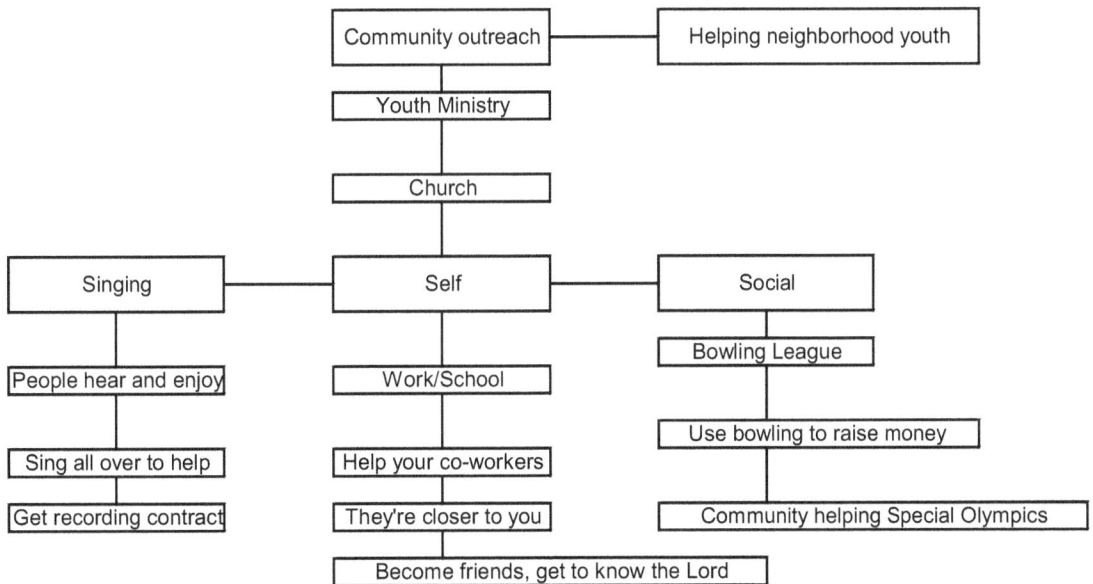

```
Community outreach ———— Helping neighborhood youth
        |
  Youth Ministry
        |
     Church
        |
Singing ———— Self ———— Social
   |           |          |
People hear    Work/School  Bowling League
and enjoy      |            |
   |        Help your     Use bowling to raise money
Sing all    co-workers      |
over to help   |         Community helping Special Olympics
   |        They're
Get         closer to you
recording
contract    Become friends, get to know the Lord
```

Current influence

Future influence, (Where you think it might be years from now.)

Your own ideas of influence

Personal Notes

Chapter 12
Trial By Fire part 3

Please read Daniel 3:13-30

"If it be so, our God whom we serve is able to deliver us from the burning fiery furnace, and He will deliver us out of thine hand, O King. But if not, be it known unto thee, O King, that we will not serve thy gods, nor worship the golden image which thou hast set up." Daniel 3:17-18

In verses 13-15 of Daniel 3, King Nebuchadnezzar, was furious with Shadrach, Meshach, and Abednego. He was close to them and now felt betrayed because they disobeyed a direct order from him. He immediately brought them in and reminded them of the laws, and then questioned the power and authority of God.

Whenever a group or person is questioning our stance for God, they are more or less questioning the authority of God. They do not believe that what God says is true and feel like what they know and say is true. When David fought Goliath, (1 Samuel 17:40-54), the Philistine giant did the exact same thing when he was about to battle David. But David came at him in the name of the Lord and fought against the man who decided to defame God and His people.

"David said to the Philistine, 'You come against me with sword and spear and javelin, but I come against you in the name of the Lord Almighty, the God of the armies of Israel, whom you have defied,'" 1 Samuel 17:45 (NIV). Remember that when someone is tearing our character apart, then they are also tearing God apart, (2 Kings 2:23-24, Matthew 25:45). It is the same if they are uplifting a person, then they are also uplifting God, (Matthew 25:40).We have to know and have the wisdom to follow what God has told us. Remember the Lord has our best interest in mind and will devour all those who speak against us. "The Lord preserveth all them that love Him: but all the wicked will He destroy," Psalms 145:20.

The three Hebrew men were facing death. They can see the furnace and the King reminds them of the law. There was no need. They knew the laws and they knew what the punishment was, but for them, to not stand for God was worse than flames and pain.

Their answer to the King was simple. "If it be so, our God whom we serve is able to deliver us from the burning fiery furnace, and He will deliver us out of thine hand, O King. But if not, be it known unto thee, O king, that we will not serve thy gods, nor worship the golden image which thou hast set up," Daniel 3:17-18.

The three Hebrew men knew that God could save them from the furnace and certain death. They knew God was greater then any person or nation. The three Hebrew men made sure to let the King know, in a very respectful way, that God will save them.

With respect, when going up against someone who is bent on trying to force us to do what he or she says, let it be known that they have no power. Not all people can say exactly what the three men said, but God will give us the words and courage. Remember that we are representing God and the trial that we are currently going through is to let others know, that God is with us. In doing that, you are allowing God to show His powers to others, which can change lives. If we fail, then God is looked upon as a failure. The Lord will not allow Himself to seem weaker than humans or any other agencies that is meant to destroy His people, and you are one of His people. "…I will place My law within them and write it on their hearts. I will be their God, and they will be My people," Jeremiah 31:33 (HCSB).

We might be nervous or scared. The heat of the furnace made that room very uncomfortable for the three men. The sweat of their brow reminded them that this furnace would kill them if they were tossed into it. Nevertheless, they stood firm for God and never wavered in their association with Him. We can do the same. It might seem bad because they might try to fire us at our job, kick us out of the organization, or excommunicate a person from church. Stand for God, it will be hard, but stand for Him and know that by doing this we are changing lives. Not only ours but those around us.

Shadrach, Meshach, and Abednego all knew that God could save them, but if not, then they where still going to serve the Lord until death and will not give in to this image nor any other gods that King Nebuchadnezzar had. They where making it clear that nothing will sway them from God. Nothing now and nothing in the future. They did not know if the King would start to create other images or force people to worship other gods, so just in case, no means no to all future worship of various false idols.

But if not. These three words are a powerful testament of love and faith to God. Regardless of what was going to happen, Shadrach, Meshach, and Abednego would stand for God. Faith like this is easy to say, harder to do.

Imagine if we were to tell our boss, we would not work past a certain time or on a certain day because God told us not to and we will not be fired, but if they still threaten to fire us, we will still not work during those times. Telling our social organization that they will not get rid of us, but if they would then we will continue to serve all people. What if we told the church that their beliefs are false and unfounded in the Bible and God will not allow them to dis-fellowship us from the church, but if they do then we will still stand on the rock and what the Bible says and not what they tell us to believe in.

The men were not trying to become martyrs, they believed in worshipping the true God. If by representing God meant death, then so be it, but they were not going to go against God's will. They did not look for fame in being a martyr nor the lasting legacy it can bring. They were not trying to change a society nor were they even trying to change the King. All they knew was that bowing down to an image was wrong, so they decided to do what was right.

We do not have to look for ways to become a martyr. For example being fired at our job, forced out of the church, kicked out of an organization, disowned by family, or killed by the government. It is not our job to look for means of self-glorification in being a martyr. God wants us to live, and to live for Him. Jesus is a great example of someone who knew He had to die for our sins but even still was not looking to do it for His self-exaltation.

"And going a little farther, He threw Himself upon the ground on His face and prayed saying, My Father, if it is possible, let this cup pass away from Me; nevertheless, not what I will {not what I desire} but as You will and desire," Matthew 26:39 (AMP). Jesus Himself, the greatest martyr to live, die, and then live again, did not go into Calvary wanting to be exalted for self. He actually asked if it was possible to have another way of completing this mission. He knew that there were none, but was showing us the example of not going into situations where we desire to be a martyr for our own sake.

It's all about doing God's will. His work must be accomplished, not ours. To be remembered is great but to live for God is even better. There are times while living for God we might experience our own fiery furnace.

Foundation of the Fire   167

The King was furious with their response and threw them into the furnace that was turned up even higher, (Daniel 3:19-23). The heat killed the men who tossed the Israelites in, but the story does not end with the Hebrews meeting death and doom.

"Lo, I see four men loose, walking in the midst of the fire, and they have no hurt; and the form of the fourth is like the Son of God," Daniel 3:25.

The King was astonished for two reasons, He could not believe that the three Hebrew men had no hurt and that another came down into the midst of the flame and that it was the Son of God.

When we are going through trials always remember that Jesus is right there with us, (John 6:18-21). Nebuchadnezzar could see that they were up walking around in the furnace. This means that in the midst of the flames they were still moving, still praising, and still representing God. In these Macedonian furnaces, where sometimes cool spots, but by walking around in the furnace then you would immediately get out of the cool spot and into certain death.

Praise Him! Simply praise God, even in the midst of trials. Is it hard? Yes. Is it possible? Yes. Walk around and begin to show those who try to do harm that they can do no damage because Jesus is there.

In the midst of the fire, Jesus shows up and begins to intermingle with the three Hebrew men. His countenance was unmistakable to the point that the Babylonian King, full of false idol worship and gods, could see the true Son of God.

This is what God desires and wants from His people. He knows that through us, others will not only see His people make it through the trial but see Jesus alongside of us. They can begin to see for themselves just what it means to have a relationship with Christ. The Son of God was right there the entire time. The three Hebrew men knew that Jesus would be there for them, and now the King saw what they knew the entire time.

God is in our life, but often others cannot see nor feel His presence. When they think they are mistreating us, our response will allow them to see God. Do not worry about whether or not harm will come to you. Even in the fire, the King could see that no harm was on them, but it became reality when they stepped out of the furnace.

"And the princes, governors, and captains, and the king's counsellors, being gathered together, saw these men, upon whose bodies the fire had no power, nor was an hair of their head singed, neither were their coats changed, nor the smell of fire had passed on them," Daniel 3:27.

This shows how the world has no power over God. What He wants will go according to His way. The fire had no power, because Jesus showed up and took the heat out of the fire. What would normally destroy a man became the means of obliterating the ropes tied around them. The very trial that the King used to kill them ended up removing the restraints that were on their lives.

God will remove all restraints that are stopping His people from being able to live for Him. The Lord will not continue to allow us to be restrained because it stops His work for the world. Whatever the trial might be, God can use that fire to remove that which is holding us back. Pray and allow Him access so that you no longer have any ropes, chains, or anything else stopping the mission from being accomplished.

Three specific aspects are mentioned when those who go through the trial come out because the fire had no ill effect on them.

1.) Their hair and how it was not singed. Our minds, like theirs, will not be affected. The same belief we have going to the fire we will still have coming out. God will protect our minds so it is not warped and confused.

2.) The clothes they wore were untouched. Our likeness and appearance should be unchanged. The Lord cares about what we look like, because He made us. Right now we are what God want us to look like. God desires the best for us and wants to make sure that we always shine for Him. If we care about our looks and the perception that people get from us, then so does God. He knows that at our best we are able to serve Him more effectively.

3.) There was not even the hint of smoke on them. Nothing the king did could last. When going through a trial the lasting reminder of us going through something awful will not stay around. The smell of smoke or the smell of burning will not be there because we did not burn. Sure, we went through the trial but we were not affected by it. The only change that took place was the bonds being broken and the king's mindset being changed.

Now not only does the king notice the men but also other people in high places and officials saw the amazement of Christ in the three Hebrew men's lives. By standing up for God, we show others what it means to be under the protection and authority of the Lord. Those who try to go against the Lord's people and try to set us up for failure like in Daniel 3:8-12, can now see the error of their ways.

The ministry God has given us will change not only us but also those we meet. God believes in reaching all people. From those who are the lowest in society to the ones with the greatest power. God believes in touching all people, because just like Nebuchadnezzar making the image and forcing everybody to worship, so will the same King go about to make leeway to give all people the opportunity to worship the one true God. By reaching leaders, hundreds, and sometimes thousands of people will follow. Be the person to guide people in the right direction to God.

You could be that leader, not in the dishing out of trials, but by directing people to God. We all have some purpose or mission to do for the Lord. It varies in work and area, people and means. However, we all have something to do for God, and going through trials of this sort pushes people around you to change and recognize that truly God is the all-powerful authoritative figure that He says He is.

Building a foundation in God will allow you to get through these circumstances unharmed and having no ill effect. God does not want to harm you, but make sure that you can be the best witness for Him. Stand for God; watch Him make miracles in your life. People's lives will be changed because God is dwelling in you and they will see it, and will want God to show up in their lives as well. You just have to show them that it is okay, and give them the example that showing up for Christ can make all the difference in the world.

The only way you can accomplish this is by building a strong foundation in God.

Quoted Scripture

Daniel 3:17-18 Our God whom we serve is able to deliver us
1 Samuel 17:45 I come against you in the name of the Lord Almighty (NIV)
Psalms 145:20 The Lord preserveth all them that love Him
Jeremiah 31:33 I will place My law within them and write it on their hearts (HCSB)
Matthew 26:39 My Father, if it is possible, let this cup pass away from Me (AMP)
Daniel 3:25 Lo, I see four men loose, walking in the midst of the fire
Daniel 3:27 Saw these men, upon whose bodies the fire had no power

Scripture for Future Study

1 Samuel 17:40-54 David battles Goliath
2 Kings 2:23-24 Youth begin to make fun of God's prophet
Daniel 3:13-30 The three men stand up for God and against Nebuchadnezzar false god
Matthew 25:31-46 Difference between those who help others and people who do not

STUDY GUIDE

1.)   What was King Nebuchadnezzar reaction after Shadrach, Meshach, and Abednego
        choose not to bow down to the image?
Daniel 3:13-15; FOTF Pg 165

2.)   The King not only questions the ideals of the three men, but the authority of God.
        This happens elsewhere in the Bible. Read 1 Samuel 17:40-54 and describe the
        account that happens there. What was the fate of the person who questioned God's
        authority?

3.)   After the King reminded the three Hebrew men of the death sentence what was their
        response?
Daniel 3:17-18; FOTF Pg 166

4.)   Why was it important for Shadrach, Meshach, and Abednego to make it clear they would not worship anything now and in the future, the king lay before them? When giving a response to an ideal that is going against God's will, should you waver or stand regardless?

5.)   "But if not", is powerful because it means even if it means death, they would not serve no earthly King. Do you feel the church today has that same ideal of it's better to die and server God then to give into the ideal of he world? Are we as Christians setting a moral code for this country or in the community you're living in?

6.)   What where the three Hebrew men trying not to become? Why would this be wrong?
FOTF Pg 167

7.)   The men are thrown into the furnace and the King is amazed. What are the two reasons for his shock and awe?
Daniel 3:25, FOTF Pg 168

8.)   Who had to proclaim that God of the three Hebrew men is God of all?
FOTF Pg 168

9.)   Can you imagine the same people who wanted to destroy you ended up changing to believe in your ways? Notice what happens when Jesus gets the glory. What example can you give that will reflect this same sentiment?

10.)   When getting out of the furnace, three aspects are mention in that no ill effect came
        upon the men. List the ways and how this relates to people when coming out of trials?
FOTF Pg 169

11.)   What can you be for the Lord?
FOTF Pg 170

12.)   What should you do?
FOTF Pg 170

PERSONAL STUDY

1.)   Because the three Hebrew men stood for God, the Lord was revealed in the midst of the fire. Why would God show up in the midst of a struggle and how are you comforted in knowing that God is there in hard times?

2.)   When the men left the furnace, no harm was on them. Describe how a trial/struggle can leave no scars on our character/personality and how can this experience help us to help others?

3.)   How can the three Hebrew men look at the furnace, which was earth, and possibly tell the King that they would not worship the image he created? What lessons can we learn as a society or church that we can do what God says and bend to outside influences?

ACTIVITY

By now, you are on the road in building a relationship with God. This the beginning but continue on. For the last activity, write out how you can be of use for the Lord and what you can do to be of service for Him.

Pray for an opportunity to be a representative and when something comes along then do it. Write out a personal journal to keep track of your daily progress. This way you can see your self grow in Christ and you can comment on how you've changed as well as realize that God has been blessing you all along.

Personal Notes

The Conclusion

Please read 2 Timothy 2:15-19

"Nevertheless, God's solid foundation stands firm, sealed with this inscription: 'The Lord knows those who are His'..." 2 Timothy 2:19 (NIV)

God is desirous of all people to build a strong foundation in Him. The journey through this life can become a rewarding one and full of peace. The time will come eventually when God will begin to separate His people from those who do not choose Him. Having a knowledge of God is a start, but it will not get us into Heaven. Remember "Thou believest that there is one God; thou doest well: the devils also believe, and tremble," James 2:19. We have to take it beyond merely knowing about God, and build in Him a firm foundation with trust that He will guide our lives.

Jesus is currently revealing Himself to us. He is allowing us to get to know who He is and has guided our lives so that we will freely come to Him. There is joy where Christ is and He desires to build a relationship with everyone. The Lord has a special blessing waiting for us to come and receive what He is offering.

The life that He has prepared is more precious than gold or platinum. He has already tried it through the fire and knows that if we keep our eyes on Him and the goals of Heaven then nothing can stop us. Our blessing is on the way. We have to develop a communication with God.

By studying the Bible, praying, singing, praises and all type of other communication, we begin to build a relationship with God. During the time of conversing with the Lord, we begin to build up strong emotions and love for the Master Creator. God will reveal Himself to us but we have to trust Him with our lives and know that there are areas He has to fix.

Believing that we can do any evil we want and God will be okay with it, is faulty thinking. God loves us and knows what is best. He desires to come into our lives and remove all sin and the mess, which can block us from being the best possible person we can be. The preparation process that we must go through is so He can send us into the world to fulfill our destiny.

God has already set up within each person the skills, talents, and abilities to complete His will. He has a special mission that is personal for each person. Our life experiences, aspirations, talents, residency, and the period we are currently living in has all been weighed, measured, and tested. Jesus guarantees success for us to do the work of the Lord. So let our personal light shine, because darkness is all around and many people need to see.

By the power of the Holy Spirit, our light will be able to bring about change to whomever we meet. Jesus, through the Holy Ghost, will work marvelous things in our lives. He constantly revealing the truth about our Lord and Savior and always giving us more than enough power to be able to overcome anything. All we have to do is show up to wherever God calls us and allow the process of the Holy Spirit to work on our hearts.

We might go through trials but always remember that Jesus is right there with us in the fire. Study the scriptures and learn what God has in store for you. By standing for Christ, great things will come about. Leaders will have to listen, churches will have to believe, family members will begin to reconsider, and complete strangers will follow. Tribulations will come but God will use those life trials as fire and mold us to be better than we can imagine. We will step out of the furnace unscathed and only the bonds that the world try to force on us will be removed.

God will not force you to love Him but will do all He can to bring you to His side. Not because He wants to win some bet against the Devil, but because He loves you and has a home in Heaven waiting for your presence. The choice is yours. Listen, follow the teachings of God, and allow Him to anchor you to the Rock or build your home in the sand. Which choice will you choose today to build your foundation?

Quoted Scripture Index

Book	Chapter/Verses	Book Chapter	Version
Genesis	1:1	Seven	KJV
Exodus	3:2	Two	KJV
Exodus	3:5	Two	NLT
Exodus	25:21-22	Four	KJV
Deuteronomy	8:3	Introduction	NLV
1 Samuel	17:45	Twelve	NIV
2 Samuel	22:2	Introduction	KJV
Psalm	22:1	Four	KJV
Psalm	27:2	One	KJV
Psalm	27:1	Eleven	KJV
Psalm	30:5	Seven	KJV
Psalm	51:5	Five	KJV
Psalm	104:4	One	KJV
Psalm	145:20	Twelve	KJV
Isaiah	5:20	Five	KJV
Isaiah	43:2	Ten	NCV
Isaiah	54:17	One	KJV
Isaiah	55:1	Three	AMP
Jeremiah	1:8	Four	KJV
Jeremiah	20:7-8	Four	CEV
Jeremiah	20:8	Four	KJV
Jeremiah	20:9	Four	KJV
Jeremiah	31:33	Four	KJV
Jeremiah	31:33	Eleven	NCV
Jeremiah	31:33	Twelve	HCSB
Ezekiel	18:32	One	KJV
Ezekiel	18:32	Seven	NLV
Daniel	3:17-18	Twelve	KJV
Daniel	3:25	Twelve	KJV
Daniel	3:27	Twelve	KJV
Hosea	4:6	Four	KJV
Malachi	2:17	Five	KJV
Malachi	3:2	Six	KJV
Matthew	3:11	Eight	KJV
Matthew	3:17	Eight	KJV
Matthew	5:14	Seven	KJV
Matthew	6:19-20	Three	KJV
Matthew	6:33	Three	KJV
Matthew	7:15	Ten	KJV
Matthew	9:12-13	Introduction	KJV

Matthew	11:28	Introduction	KJV
Matthew	24:14	Seven	KJV
Matthew	26:39	Twelve	AMP
Matthew	27:46	Four	KJV
Mark	15:34	Four	KJV
Luke	6:46-47	Introduction	Message
Luke	6:48-49	Introduction	KJV
John	1:6-8	Seven	KJV
John	3:3	Eight	KJV
John	13:35	One	KJV
John	16:13	Three	KJV
John	16:13-14	Nine	KJV
Acts	1:8	Nine	KJV
Romans	1:21-23	Five	KJV
Romans	1:28	Five	KJV
Romans	1:32	Five	KJV
Romans	6:23	Five	KJV
1 Corinthians	10:4	Introduction	KJV
1 Corinthians	13:11	Four	KJV
2 Corinthians	5:7	Three	KJV
Galatians	4:3-5	One	CEV
Galatians	5:22-23	Nine	KJV
2 Timothy	2:19	Conclusion	
Hebrews	5:13-14	Four	KJV
Hebrews	10:26-27	Five	KJV
Hebrews	12:25-29	Introduction	KJV
James	1:22	Introduction	KJV
James	2:19	Conclusion	
2 Peter	3:9	Introduction	KJV
1 John	1:5	Nine	KJV
1 John	4:8	Three	YLT
Revelations	3:17	Three	KJV
Revelations	3:18	Three	KJV

LaVauri Publishing House

www.lavauri.com

Inspirational Books Available For Sale in Paperback and Kindle (e-book) versions

In The Beginning – A 26 Lesson Study on the book of Genesis. It covers all 50 chapters in twenty-six lessons that are designed for learning and application. Ash lesson is divided into two sections. Part one covers the chapters directly from the Bible whereas part two allows for deeper thinking and applying the knowledge on a personal level.

The Golden Image – From the Oceanside city of Sheridan Falls are thirteen stories based on its various citizens. Each person has a unique narrative to tell that is inspired by a story from the Bible. All stories are interconnected and lead to the title story and anchor of the book, "The Golden Image." Tales of strength, courage, overcoming, and determination are displayed by the citizens and young people of Sheridan Falls.

For more information regarding this book
(videos, events, other information)

Go to:

http://www.lavauri.com/foundation

Thank you for your support

www.ingramcontent.com/pod-product-compliance
Lightning Source LLC
Chambersburg PA
CBHW080154070426
42447CB00037B/3401